WHAT NUMBER
ARE YOU?

By the same author:

WHAT COLOUR ARE YOU?
Lilla Bek and Annie Wilson

WHAT NUMBER ARE YOU?

Lilla Bek
and
Robert Holden

Aquarian/Thorsons
An Imprint of HarperCollinsPublishers

The Aquarian Press
An Imprint of HarperCollins*Publishers*
77–85 Fulham Palace Road,
Hammersmith, London w6 8jb

Published by The Aquarian Press 1992
10 9 8 7 6 5 4 3 2

© Lilla Bek and Robert Holden 1992

Lilla Bek and Robert Holden assert the moral right to
be identified as the authors of this work

A catalogue record for this book
is available from the British Library

isbn 1 85538 135 4

Printed in Great Britain by HarperCollins Manufacturing, Glasgow

CONTENTS

CHAPTER ONE

THE ANCIENT SCIENCE OF NUMEROLOGY

The mathematicians of ancient times often described numbers as symbols of cosmic and divine opportunity. They considered numbers not as lifeless digits but as living symbols of energy, character and potential. Ancient mathematicians maintained and it continues to be believed that behind each and every number there exists specific potentials that can profoundly influence and affect your personal growth and development. Furthermore, it is believed that the numbers in your life appear by plan and by providence. Your numbers are, therefore, highly significant to you.

The mathematicians and scientists of modern times would certainly not, for the most part, counsel or entertain the idea that numbers have a personal potential that can influence human consciousness and all life. And yet, when we look at our common everyday language there are words, phrases and idioms that may suggest something different. These linguistic landmarks are, perhaps, the remnants of an old and almost forgotten wisdom—a wisdom that taught *'All is arranged according to number.'*

Very often we will use the word *number* to describe character and personality. We say, for instance, 'I've got their number' to mean that we understand a person. We may also describe someone who is difficult to get along

with as a 'tricky number'. Also, when we have good
fortune we have a phrase for it: we say, 'My number has
come!' And when we have bad fortune, we say 'My
number is up.'

We also often use the word number to describe our
actions and performances. 'He did his number on me
again' can be translated as 'He's playing his old games
again' or 'He was true to his character, once again.' 'That
was a nice number' is sometimes said to mean 'That was a
nice performance.' 'What a number!' might mean 'What a
trick!' And 'Here comes a number' is a bit like 'Here comes
a card', which means to say, 'Here comes a character.'

Every person upon our Planet has a unique arrangement
of numbers in his or her life. The study of numerology
insists that this arrangement is not an arbitrary, aimless
affair, but rather a living, meaningful power and potential.
The mathematicians of ancient times were convinced that
a pattern of purpose and providence rests behind every
personal set of numbers. 'Numbers are not lucky,' they
said; 'Numbers are not lifeless: numbers are lessons,' they
proclaimed, 'and the lessons are alive.'

Numbers: A Philosophy

It is as if the very first Breath of God sent a stream of
numbers into infinite space and infinite time, and that
upon those numbers there settled a world and a life that we
are now privileged to experience. This is how Pythagoras,
the Father of Mathematics, envisaged the mystical Dawn
of Creation. He believed that,

> From the monad came the indeterminate duad; from
> them came numbers; from numbers, points; from
> points, lines; from lines, superfices; from superfices,

solids; from these, solid bodies, whose elements are four: viz., fire, water, air, earth; all of which, under various transmutations, the world consists.

The contemplatives and thinkers of ancient times were the first to develop a science of numbers for the world of material form and physical phenomena. It became known as *the Mother of All Sciences*, and as *the first science*. The sciences of travel, astronomy, economics, trade, architecture, geometry, chemistry, alchemy, physics—and, indeed, every other science—owe their foundations and support to the science of numbers.

The great minds of ancient times were, however, equally interested in the pursuit of an inner, poetic and philosophical meaning of numbers. Their study was the philosophy of numbers, today referred to most often as *numerology*. The philosophy of numbers described numbers as Cosmic Potencies that have essentially two faces, or two meanings: the outward face is for physical sciences; the inward face is for philosophy—and it is this inner meaning that defines numbers as symbols of innate character, universal influences and personal potential.

The records of the historian, the theologian and the archaeologist, for instance, are replete with evidence and examples of how the contemplatives and philosophers of ancient civilizations and cultures, such as the Greek, Babylonian, Phoenician, Hebrew, Celtic, Egyptian, Mayan and Tibetan, each independently evolved a philosophical system of numbers to describe and explain 'the thoughts of God' and 'the heartbeats of Nature'.

The mathematician of ancient times believed that *the deeper you look into a number, the more you can see of the whole world*. Thus, the mathematics of ancient times was as much a philosophy as it was a physical science. The priest of the day would, therefore, probably have been most conversant with numbers. So too, however, would the geometrician of the day have been well acquainted with poetry; the chemist (or alchemist) with philosophy; and the astronomer with priesthood. This is because of an innate belief, held first by peoples of ancient times, that there is both a scientific and philosophic truth and meaning to all things.

Today we are witnessing the dawn of a 'whole-brain' and 'whole-person' approach to science which openly acknowledges the importance of an inner, poetic and philosophical meaning. Nowhere is this more true than in the study of quantum physics. Quantum physicists such as the German Nobel Prize winner Max Planck now feel free to say things like, 'Science…means unresting endeavour and continually progressing development toward an aim which the poetic intuition may apprehend, but which the intellect can never fully grasp.'

Mathematics is no longer a cold and lifeless science, seeking only to divide and separate. Indeed, as the English scientist and psychologist Havelock Ellis once said, 'Here, where we reach the sphere of mathematics, we are among processes which seem to some the most inhuman of all human activities and the most remote from poetry. Yet it is here that the artist has the fullest scope of his imagination.'

A Sacred Science

> Behind the wall, the gods play; they play with numbers, of which the Universe is made up.
>
> *Le Corbusier*

The philosophers and mathematicians of ancient Greece, such as Pythagoras, Xeno, Plato and Aristotle, were among the first to attribute a great and precise sanctity to numbers—particularly the first ten integers. They believed in a *Doctrine of Numbers* which they described as 'the language of God'. This language was, they believed, communicated to them in their meditations through celestial bodies, or 'agents of God'.

Numbers were thought to be symbols for the building bricks and the fabrics of Creation. They represented the archetypes through which the unmanifest could manifest, the infinite could become finite, the implicate could become the explicate, and the spiritual could become earthed in matter. A study of numbers was considered, therefore, to be a study of God and of God's Creation. The study of numbers was a truly sacred science.

A study of the world's religious and philosophical texts and scriptures shows how many cultures and civilizations of ancient times came to an apparently similar conclusion. Throughout Asia, for instance, numbers were revered as 'of the kind of Brahma', and also as 'of the bodies of Brahma'. The numbers from sixty down to one were reserved by the Babylonians for a particular deity. Jewish students of the Qabalah devised their own Doctrine of Numbers, referred to as *gematria*.

Mystical rites, spiritual rituals and sacred initiations, as practised by the Celts and the Gnostics, for instance, were often based upon the divine power of numbers. And as one noted Egyptian historian once pointed out, 'A large portion of the Egyptian philosophy and religion seems to have been constructed almost wholly upon the science of numbers...everything in Nature was explained on this principle alone.' By the 1st century AD, a system of numerology similar to that of Pythagoras was also current in the Kingdom of China.

The Bible has its own Book of Numbers in The Old Testament, the symbolic meaning of which has fascinated numerologists and theologians alike throughout the centuries. There are also references to numbers in other parts of the Bible. In the Book of Ezekiel, for instance, there is a passage which reads, 'God hath numbered thy Kingdom, and finished it.' It is well known, also, that St Augustine, the first archbishop of Canterbury, was fascinated by and devoted much of his life to the ecclesiastical symbolism of numbers. Indeed, wherever one looks the study of numbers and the study of God have often stood side by side.

Rhythms, Cycles and Vibrations

> That which goes out of being also comes into being; and that which comes into being also goes out of being.
>
> *Hermes*

Humanity's early preoccupation with numbers seems to have stemmed from the observation of the rhythms of days and nights, the phases of the Moon, the journey of the Sun, the turning of the tides and the seasons of the year. To the numerologist, life is supported by and evolves through cycles upon cycles upon cycles. Linear time, which is the time of sequences and of beginnings and of ends, is dismissed as the *Time of Man*; Cyclic time is proclaimed as the *Time of God*.

The ancient philosophers and mathematicians also described our world as a dynamic, creative and free-flowing river of energies and life forces. Every person you meet, every place you visit, every object you see and touch, be it a plant or a tree, a crystal or a stone, is a unique arrangement and expression of this energy. All is vibration. Vibration is life.

Numbers stand as symbols for these vibrations, or

Creation Energies. For the numerologist they represent the streams of potential which feed, support and influence the Universe, and help it evolve. These streams course through space by way of short and long, and small and enormous, cycles of time.

A belief in the twin existence of *Cyclic Time* and a *Dynamic Universe* are cornerstones of the ancient philosophers' and mathematicians' understanding of numbers. It is indeed exciting and most gratifying to find that the modern scientist and mathematician is also beginning to give credence to these ideas. In his book *Mind Over Matter*, Kit Pedler promotes the perceptions of a new physics which describes Creation as a dynamic, dancing universal flow of unified life-energy. He writes,

> The view of Nature now proposed by physics is a much more mobile, flowing whole. The fixed mechanistic world of Newton has given way to a view that is more broadly based, but just as logical and rational. It is a view which only talks about flowing interactions and connections and not about rigidly locked structures in a fixed and motionless space and time.

Microcosm and Macrocosm

> Man is a microcosm, or a little world, because he is an extract from all the stars and planets of the whole firmament, from the earth and the elements; and so he is their quintessence.
>
> *Paracelsus*

While the origin of numerology may have evolved from the study of the vast cosmic and universal cycles which weave across space and time, the development of numerology has focused more and more on the personal cycles, rhythms, seasons and tides within us which influence, effect and determine our own evolution.

The ancient philosophers and mathematicians played with the idea of 'microcosm-macrocosm', i.e. that *within every macrocosm there are microcosms, and within every micro-cosm therein rests the macrocosm.* In other words, each person on this Planet is a miniature world (microcosm) living in the Universe (macrocosm), but, at the same time, the Universe (macrocosm) lives within us (microcosm). *Therefore, that which supports, feeds and changes the Universe, must also support, feed and change us.*

The philosophic and poetic texts of the world support this idea of 'microcosm-macrocosm'. One of the Bibles of the East, *The Upanishads*, contains a wonderful description of the human spirit. It reads,

> This is the Spirit that is in my heart, smaller than a grain of rice, or a grain of barley, or a grain of mustard-seed, or a grain of canary seed, or the kernel of a grain of canary-seed. This is the Spirit that is in my heart, greater than the earth, greater than the sky, greater than heaven itself, greater than all these worlds.

Once again, it is interesting to note that the modern scientist and mathematician also now pays credence to the idea of 'microcosm-macrocosm'. The physicist Max Planck once wrote,

> According to modern mechanics [field theory] each individual particle of the system, in a certain sense, at any one time, exists simultaneously in every part of the space occupied by the system. The simultaneous exist-ence applies not merely to the field of force with which it is surrounded, but also its mass and its charge.

Some modern biologists share a similar belief: they believe that a single plant cell carries within it the capability to reproduce the entire plant. Commenting on this breakthrough, Gary Zukav, author of *The Dancing Wu Li Masters*, wrote,

> Similarly, the philosophical implication of quantum mechanics is that all of the things in our Universe (including us) that appear to exist independently, are actually parts of one all-encompassing organic pattern, and that no parts of that pattern are ever really separate from it or from each other.

The numerologists of ancient times believed that not only do the powers represented by numbers support, influence and affect Planets, Moons, Suns and Galaxies, but also the life-forms upon these worlds. In other words, your evolution, your progress and your life also have a profound and influential relationship with numbers. *Your life is numbered.*

Masculine and Feminine Numbers

> The way begets one; the one begets two; the two begets three; three begets the myriad creatures. The myriad creatures carry on their backs the yin [feminine] and embrace in their arms the yang [masculine] and are the blend of the generative forces of the two.
>
> *Tao te Ching*

The philosopher and mathematician of almost every ancient civilization and culture believed that the essential, universal forces which continually support, recreate and affect the evolution of the world, as symbolized by numbers, can be divided into two fundamentally opposing yet complementary natures of *masculine* and *feminine*. Thus, odd numbers, such as one, three, five, seven and nine were described as having a masculine influence; whereas even numbers, such as two, four, six and eight, were described as having a feminine influence. The ancient numerologists held the belief that the universe and everything in it is made up of a dual nature of both masculine and feminine, active and passive, initiating and supportive, introvert and extrovert, yin and yang.

Masculine	Feminine
Yang	Yin
Animus	Anima
Sun	Moon
Light	Dark
Warm	Cool
Expansive	Contractive
Intellect	Intuition
Logic	Imagination
Individual	Collective
Active	Passive
Initiate	Sustaining

Many of the world's best known mythologies, legends, religions and philosophies support the idea of a universal dance between masculine and feminine. The 'Father Sky' and 'Mother Earth' of the North American Indians; the 'Lord of Sky' and 'Lady of Earth' of the Maori tradition; the 'He Gods', 'She Gods', and 'He-She Gods' of Egypt; the 'Gods' and 'Goddesses' of Greece; and even the Adam and Eve story of the Old Testament, are just a few of the many examples from around the world which express this innate belief in a masculine and feminine framework to the life and to the existence we are witness to.

The modern mathematician and scientist is also fascinated by the theory of opposites. Once again, modern physics leads the way with its work in symmetry and polarity; in anti-matter and anti-worlds; and in electrons, protons and neutrons. The famous Danish physicist Niels Bohr, a Nobel Prize winner, was so enthralled by the play of opposites in life that he designed his own coat-of-arms around the ancient yin-yang symbol.

Fritjof Capra explains the current thinking of modern physicists:

> The basic force...which gives rise to all atomic phenomena is familiar and can be experienced in the macroscopic world. It is the force of electric attraction between the positively charged atomic nucleus and the negatively charged electrons. The interplay of this force with the electron waves gives rise to the tremendous variety of structures and phenomena in our environment. It is responsible for all chemical reactions, and for the formation of molecules, that is, of aggregates of several atoms bound to each other by mutual attraction. The interaction between electrons [negatives] and atomic nuclei [positives] is thus the basis of all solids, liquids and gases, and also of all living organisms and of the biological processes associated with them.

> *The Tao of Physics*, pages 82–3

Replace the words *positive* and *negative* with *masculine* and *feminine* and it would appear that the ancient philosopher and the modern scientist share a similar view of a world created and evolving through the plays and the dances of two opposing yet complementary natures. This relationship provides the basis for each and every relationship that there ever has been and that there ever will be.

'Lucky' and 'Unlucky' Numbers

> Good luck lies in odd numbers...They say, there is divinity in odd numbers, either in nativity, chance or death.
>
> *William Shakespeare, The Merry Wives of Windsor*,
> V.i.

Every system of numerology in the ancient world had its so-called 'lucky' and 'unlucky' numbers. Most often the 'lucky' numbers were so-called because of an intimate connection to a Deity, an association with Nature, or a mathematical relationship with music.

The number two was considered by almost every arithmetic tradition to be the most fatal and 'unlucky' of numbers, representing division, diversity, strife, disorder, conflict and opposition: 'It takes two to make a quarrel.' The number three was considered by almost every arithmetic tradition to be the most 'lucky' and prosperous of numbers, representing perfect harmony, light and the healing of division and diversity. The number three also represented the Trinity as found in so many world faiths: 'All good things come in threes.'

In the ancient Oriental numerology traditions, the number five, for example, was considered 'lucky' because that number is abundant in Nature, such as in the Five Elements (earth, fire, water, air and wood) and in the Five Viscera, or internal organs, of the body. The theorists of music and harmonics worked with a scale of Five Tones. And then there was also the Five Virtues of the Confucians (humanity, righteousness, morality, fidelity and trust-worthiness).

In the Pythagorean system of arithmetic, the number five was 'lucky' because it was considered to be the prevailing number in Nature. Indeed, all odd numbers were thought to be 'lucky' and 'holy' numbers. In the ancient arithmetic traditions of the Qabalah, five was considered 'lucky' because of its association with a symbol, the Star of David or five-pointed star. And yet, by contrast, in Christian Ecclesiastical numerology five was a sombre number because of its link to the wounds of the Redeemer: two in the hands, two in the feet, and one in the side.

Very often a 'lucky' number in one system of numerology was believed to hold 'unlucky' powers and connotations by another. All systems of numerology seemed to agree, though, that in reality there is *both* a 'pleasant' and 'harmful' latent potential behind every number. In other words, within every number there are the seeds of failure or success, and that ultimately the choice is yours as to whether you will allow the potential behind a number to work for you or against you. Very often the deciding factor between 'good luck' and 'bad luck' rests with your efforts and your endeavours to create a world of balance, order and harmony within yourself.

Harmony

It is not for the Sun to overtake the Moon, nor doth the night outstrip the day. They float each in an orbit.

The Koran

Numbers are not separate, individual or isolated units; they are expressions of a single, far greater whole. The art of numerology, therefore, is not to operate with one or two numbers alone. Rather, it is to work with all the numbers there are, and thereby to manifest within you and around you greater harmony, greater enlightenment and greater potential. One of the highest truths of numerology is that *you are all numbers; you have infinite potential.*

The ancient numerologists also insisted that the stronger your sense of self- and inner-harmony, the better you would be able co-operate with the cycles and rhythms, motions, movements, tides and influences of life, as portrayed and characterized by numbers. *Ultimately, we study numerology to fit in, to synchronize and to make peace—with both the world around us and the world within us.*

Synchronicity is a fundamental tenet of numerological lore. To the numerologist there is no chance, no coincidence and no luck in life; rather, the world revolves around plan, providence and purpose. Therefore, the patterns and arrangements of numbers in your life are meaningful landmarks for lessons, potentials and opportunities. To synchronize and to live in tune with the numbers of your life is the highest teaching, the highest aim and the highest reward of living by numbers.

Physical, mental, emotional and spiritual harmony were considered the passports to progress, to peace and to personal liberation. This essential, inner harmony, on every level of your being, was considered to be the overriding aim of numerology. It was also considered to be the highest reward that is offered to a person who undertakes a conscious, day-to-day relationship with numbers.

Self-Knowledge

The knowledge of Self is the essential knowledge: it gives knowledge to humanity. In the understanding of

the human being lies that understanding of Nature
which reveals the law of creation.

Hazrat Inayat Khan

The deeper a person contemplates, meditates, looks into
and gets to know the essence of a number, the deeper that
person also gets to know the essence of his or her Self.
Numerology, like its sister science astrology, was considered to be essentially a Science of Self. Indeed, the
numerologist deemed all subjects and studies to be, ultimately, Studies of the Self.

Through the study of numbers we embark upon the
study of ourselves. Numbers are like cosmic clues. They
shed conscious light upon our unconscious darkness.
Strengths and weaknesses, attributes and challenges, assets
and failings—they can all become clear and they can all be
nurtured and developed or overcome and adjusted
through a conscious, day-to-day relationships with
numbers.

Through the study of numbers we also realize something of our unlimited potential. The energies which
amalgamated to create and to manifest Suns, Galaxies and
Universes are the very same energies which have amalgamated to create and to manifest ourselves. Through numbers we discover our place in a world of all possibilities.

Through the study of numbers we can, thereby, forge a
stronger, more creative and more real relationship with
ourself and with others. Thus, as well as being a sacred
philosophy of the world around us, numerology is a
personal science of our own nature and our own inner Self.

CHAPTER TWO

NUMBER PROFILES

Each and every number in your life is a symbol for a highly charged potency of energy, character, influence and opportunity. Numbers have a personality that promotes particular potentials, possibilities and probabilities, all of which you can choose either to work with or to ignore. The key to your relationship with these potentials is that *numbers work for you when you work for numbers. Or, to put it another way, numbers work when you work.*

Numerological lore subscribes to synchronicity and to providence; it completely rejects coincidence and chance. Therefore, every major number in your life, such as your *personal birthdate number* and your *personal year number*, has a precise link, connection and relationship to you. This intimate relationship operates continually on many levels of conscious and unconscious awareness, helping the shape, form and evolution of your life.

Your character, personality and experiences of life may all be inspired and influenced by the innate properties and potentials of the numbers that live with you. In other words, *the character of your numbers may inspire the character of your life.* Inspiration and influence does not, however, extend to domination or control. Numbers do not govern you, nor can they control you. *Numbers are potentials: you are the creator and the controller.*

The full potential of any number has nine dimensions to it. They are: the physical, emotional/soul, mental, will, collective, wisdom, love, spiritual, and law. All of these dimensions of potential may blossom and flower throughout your life if you will first open up to and operate on the proper levels.

One

The power and potential of the number one is linked traditionally to the vibrations of the colour red. Therefore, *red people* and *number one people* often share similar characteristics and attributes. They can be very warm, dynamic and lively people who have many natural, flowing, charming qualities. On the other hand, they can sometimes be *hot-headed*, *red-blooded* and *fiery*. On a good day number one people make first-class company and excellent companionship. On a bad day, Beware of the Bull!

The number one is also traditionally associated with the physical body. It is a number which represents manifestation, and, in particular, the impregnation of spirit into matter. The numerological history of Creation states that the first objective of God, the Creator, was to make the world appear, and that to do this God had to invoke the power and potential of the number one.

The power and potential of the number one is also connected with a day of the week: Monday, in keeping with being 'the first of'. In sacred geometry, one is linked to the Greek primordial *Monad*, which, when interpreted, means 'Divine Fire', 'Divine Spark' or 'Logos of Life'. In other words, the Monad represents the first dawn of Creation, the beginning of life for all the Galaxies, all the worlds and all life. Very often the Monad is symbolized as the dot at the exact centrepoint of the cross, itself a symbol of life in many civilizations and cultures of our world.

In astrology, the power of one is associated in particular with the Sun and to Mars, and also to the signs Aries ('I am') and Taurus ('I have'). In sacred anatomy the number one has a precise relationship with all the centres of sacred energy, called *chakras*, in the body. In particular it is connected with the red base chakra, often described as the *Chakra of Physical Life* and as *the Chakra of Reproduction and Procreation*; it is also linked with the yellow solar plexus chakra, described as the *Chakra of the Sun* and as the *Great Energy Battery Chakra*. This is interesting to note because the number one has often been associated with the Sun and with sunny personalities. Number One has also been connected with the mystical power of *kundalini* ('life-force'), and also to climax, birth and re-birth.

Assets

The power and potential of the number one is a masculine, dynamic and vibrant energy. If your personal birthdate number is a one, or if you are strongly influenced by the number one in your numerology chart, then this potential may be a source of great inspiration to you. In particular you may find that you have a great appetite for life. To a number one person, every day is the 'first day of the rest of my life'. The potential, opportunity and richness of life is sacred to a number one person.

The power and potential of the number one can often empower a person with a strong sense of direction in life. Number one people are often natural goal-setters and goal-reachers who are single-minded and single-handed in their approach. Direction is vital because it is the prerequisite for success, and success is often an absolute must for a number one person. The need to impress, to be liked, to be appreciated and to be perceived as a success are often top priorities.

The number one potential offers bravery, courage and boundless determination. Number one people are often, therefore, valiant, daring pioneers and explorers in their chosen fields of life. They are the igniters of spirit, vital, dynamic and quick, both in thought and deed. Enterprise, progress and risk are the spice of life. Discipline, enthusiasm and zest for what you do comes on tap. You may have experienced an innate awareness and consciousness that reminds you, again and again, that your potential is unlimited. It may also feel to you as if this innate awareness and consciousness has been with you for all of your life.

If you are a number one, or if you are strongly influenced by the number one in your chart, then this potential may inspire the creative, natural leader in you. You may find that you are easily self-motivated and that you can pass this motivation on to others. Number one people can be quick, clear, concise and independent thinkers who are good at decision-making, problem-solving and the giving of advice. They can also be natural motivators and influential mentors who heat up people around them. Dejection, despair and occasional laziness are only temporary blips on an otherwise hopeful, optimistic and determined approach and outlook on life.

The number one potential tends to promote invention, creativity and originality. Number one people often display 'one and only' (i.e. unique) attributes. Independence of thought and action are also hallmarks of the number one potential. So too is innocence. It is interesting to note how often a number one person displays a fresh, youthful, childlike innocence. This innocent, unique perception may be the key to your success, for it is what makes you different from others.

In full balance, a number one person will feel a strong sense of being at one with him- or herself, and with others.

They become, to borrow a phrase from Jung, *individuated*, with a strong sense of wholeness, identity and belonging. This is the basis for essentially very strong, sound and committed one-on-one relationships. The number one inspires loyalty, support, commitment and love for the people in your life, and there is an emphasis on physical attraction and sensual expression within your close relationships.

The number one is at once a most physical, material potential and also a most spiritual, poetic potential. The Oneness of life, of humanity and of Creation can be a source of great inspiration and direction for number one people. Also, the faith and belief in an omnipresent, omnipotent and omniscient God, the Creator, Who truly is Number One, may also be a guiding thought for number one people.

Challenges

An imbalanced power and potential of the number one can be decidedly dangerous. Too many number ones in your numerology chart is a potential that can, for instance, promote a selfish, self-centred and egotistical approach to life. Enormous drive and motivation is invested in being 'number one', and 'one up' on everybody. Inspiration is confused with haste; invention and insight become rebelliousness; leadership becomes dogma and domination; ambition becomes greed. Frustration, intolerance and impatience can lead to anger; whereas an increasing sense of loneliness and isolation may lead to dejection, despair and depression.

Number ones often suffer from bouts of the competitive bug. They feel they have to 'go one better' all the time. They thirst for recognition, approval and applause from others, primarily because they fail to find the same from within themselves. They are, in other words, often driven by an innate sense of inferiority. This inferiority may be caused partly by a sense of isolation. One of the essential lessons of numerology is that no number can stand on its own; one of the essential lessons of life is that no person can stand on his or her own. You cannot afford to be a 'one-man show'.

Number one people can wrap themselves up so much so in their own world that they have a fundamental lack of the natural qualities for successful, rewarding and intimate relationships, such as empathy, understanding, caring, nurturing and, at times, selflessness. It is certainly true that number ones can sometimes be guilty of being self-centred and one-sided in relationships. The ability to relate to others fully can be one of the greatest challenges for a number one person.

For all their strength and bravado, number one people can often be very vulnerable, particularly so with relationships, in which they can appear aloof, tight, unemotional and somewhat solitary. Number ones are often very independent people who need a lot of personal space and time to themselves. They can, in fact, be fiercely independent at times. As a consequence, communication of the intimate kind can often fail.

The number one can certainly promote success, but what kind of success, and at what cost? The goals of a number one person can sometimes be rather narrow ones, motivated only by personal ambition, material wealth and societal status. Success for the sake of success often brings the defeat of success. Certain types of success do not bring freedom and fulfilment; they also have a very limited lifespan. Number one people may do well to contemplate this.

One of the greatest challenges for many number one people is working on the depth and quality of their lives. Unless the shadow power of the number eight (spiritual) is allowed to empower and to influence, number one people can easily get stuck on the material and physical planes of existence. They fail to attend to the level of emotions, feelings and spirit. This can, ultimately, lead to a failure of fulfilment and an incomplete experience of individuation and wholeness.

While it is certainly true that most of the challenges of number one are normally to do with having too much and too many, very occasionally the challenges of one can also be to do with having too little or too few. Everyone will have at least one number one in their numerology chart. However, a low count of number ones can lead to certain difficulties, such as an inability to be well grounded in reality, a lack of drive, a poor sense of direction, physical frailty, unassertiveness and low ambition.

Other numbers in your full numerology chart can help to make up for a low count of number ones. For instance, the number four can help to fuel will, endeavour and drive; the number three can stimulate mental success and clear-cut direction; and the number eight, shadow of one, can provide a potential for spiritual ambition. The number one, the number of red, is, however, a base energy that is often necessary and essential for heating up the potential of all the other numbers.

Two

Traditionally the power and potential of the number two has been linked by some numerology schools with the vibrations of the colour orange, which is itself a mixture of red and yellow. Whereas the colour red symbolizes physical action and the colour yellow symbolizes the action of intellect, the colour orange unites these two forces with the action of the intuitive. The power of two is therefore an intuitive, nurturing and unifying potential.

The potential of the number two is also traditionally associated with duality, contrast and union. In geometry, two is connected with the symbol of the cross and to the caduceus (two serpents entwined around a rod), both of which are signs of duality *par excellence*. Two is, therefore, also linked with the duality of night and day, positive and negative, and, in particular, masculine and feminine.

The numerological history of the world states that at Creation, God's second objective was to divide the potential of number one so that Creation could begin to express itself in a million, million different ways. To do this God had to invoke the warm, nurturing and sustaining power of two. The cross symbol is sometimes described as a map of the world: the centrepoint is the power of one, the Monad, or Divine Spark, from which all things originate; the arms of the cross represent the power of two (vertical, masculine; horizontal, feminine) upon which all the multifarious forms of life are propagated and supported.

In sacred anatomy the number two is associated with the emotional body and also to the orange abdomen chakra and the green heart chakra. The orange chakra is sometimes described as the *Chakra of Digestion*—physical, mental and spiritual digestion. The green, heart chakra is sometimes described as the *Seat of the Soul*. In astrology the number two is connected, especially, with the day Tuesday, the Moon and the sign Cancer ('I feel').

Assets

The number two is a feminine energy which is sensitively tuned to emotion, empathy, intuition, instinct and caring. Number two people are often warm-hearted souls who make good communicators, dedicated carers, kind listeners and trustworthy mediators. They can be gentle, diplomatic, caring, understanding and sympathetic, and often present a 'good shoulder to cry on'.

The potential of number two often promotes both the honest friend and the sincere professional. For this reason, number two people are often employed in life as nurses, social workers, counsellors, occupational therapists, healers, personnel workers, receptionists and hosts. A caring person often finds his or her way into caring professions.

If you are a number two person, or if you have a strong influence of two in your numerology chart, then you may also find that you act as an unofficial agony aunt for friends, family and work colleagues. People come to you with their problems, particularly emotional problems and affairs of the heart. You are able to help, not so much because of what you do, but because of who you are.

The power of two has a very soulful quality. Number twos therefore often make deep-rooted connections with people. Their relationships can be of a most sincere and loyal nature. Romance may be very important to number two people, as well as particularly satisfying, especially if they allow the potential of seven, the shadow number, to play a part. The ability to tune in to a person, to nurture a relationship, to allow people just 'to be', and to put another person's thoughts and feelings *before one's own* are all common qualities of a well-balanced power of two.

Two is also linked to the unconscious, the instinctive and the creative. An innate need to write, dance, sing, compose, draw and especially act are qualities that are often promoted by the number two potential. Whereas the number one potential most often activates the left-brain qualities of logic, intellect, rational thought and sequential processing, the number two potential most often inspires the right-brain qualities of intuition, imagination, creativity, holistic perception and holistic processing.

Number twos often appreciate and desire harmony

above all else. The importance of home, security and stability are also very often essential priorities and attributes of a number two person. Number two people will often work hard to establish harmony, order and cohesion, both for themselves and for others, so as to achieve the resolution of conflict. They are, therefore, very often the natural healers of our world.

Challenges

People who are influenced by the power of two are often very sensitive people. This sensitivity will be either their greatest attribute or their greatest failing. Therefore, a major challenge for those of us who are influenced by the power of two is to control our emotional sensitivity. Failure to control the power of two can leave a person emotionally vulnerable for life.

Emotional conflict can dominate life for a number two person. Displays of emotional unsteadiness, such as being moody, touchy, bottled up, unpredictable, volatile and 'one minute up the next minute down' are common features of an imbalanced power of two. If you find you cannot carefully channel and control the potential of two, you may find, for instance, that rather than aiming for deep, trusting, soulful attachments, you opt instead for superficial, noncommitted emotional adventures.

One of the greatest challenges set a number two person is to spend a little less time caring for others and a little more time caring for oneself. Number two people often neglect themselves terribly. Other people's problems and other people's miseries can so often dominate their lives that they can end up putting their own lives second. The first rule of caring is that we should learn to care for ourselves. This is particularly so for those of us who are number two people or who have a significant influence of two in our numerology chart.

The number two potential can sometimes promote in you an ability to be of help to others, but, curiously enough, not the ability to be of help to yourself. Poor perspective, muddled thinking, being in 'two minds', divided loyalties, vulnerability, acting without forethought, a lack of logical reasoning, delay and procrastination are all common symptoms of imbalanced, confused misuse of the power and potential of the number two.

An absence of the number two in your numerology chart can also provoke a number of challenges, such as an inability to nurture your feminine nature, embrace your emotions, fill the soulful you and develop better empathy and understanding for others. So often having no number twos can signal suppression of emotion, repression of romance, denial of feelings for others and an absence of soul. The intuitive, creative, feminine and unconscious can all remain undiscovered and untapped.

Failure to control the power of two can leave a person lacking assertiveness, decision and control over his or her own life. Number two people are sometimes over tolerant, too accepting and very, very understanding. As a result they sometimes fail to protect and defend their own personal space. They can give out too much, and are hurt when the returns fail to measure up to the output. A failure to be independent and to live out or even to know about one's own direction, purpose and meaning in life is also very common.

A successful relationship with another person depends a lot upon the success of your own relationship with yourself. This is particularly true for people who are significantly influenced by the power of two. An uncontrolled and imbalanced power of two can leave you feeling emotionally upset and unsteady within yourself and about yourself. You may feel powerless, defenceless and openly vulnerable. You may also find that you live according to the seasons of your own turbulent and unpredictable moods and feelings. The control and influence of the number seven is often the salvation for a poorly controlled power of two.

Three

power and potential of the number three is often linked to the vibrations of yellow, which in many ancient civilizations and cultures was connected with the mind, thought and ideas. In colour healing, the vibrations of yellow are thought to stimulate and to enhance intellect, logic and rational processing. And, in the geometry of ancient times, the power and potential of three was associated with the triangle, itself a symbol of fire (yellow) and of intelligence, logic and reason.

In sacred anatomy the power and potential of the number three is linked to the mental body and also to the yellow, solar plexus chakra, sometimes referred to as the *Seat of Learning* and as the *Centre of the Sun*. Number three is also connected with the green, heart chakra (a mix of blue and yellow), a common geometric symbol for which is two interlaced triangles.

The power and potential of three corresponds in particular to the Planet Mercury (links Sun [One] and Moon [Two]), and also to the sign Virgo ('I analyse') in astrology. Three is also connected with Wednesday. In the initial Creation of the world, numerology states that God, the Creator, needed to invest the powers of consciousness and of mind into the million, million manifestations derived from the two that split the one. To do this God invoked the mental, conscious, multiplying power of three.

Assets

The power and potential of the number three promotes clear, concise, calculated thinking. It supports evaluation, analysis, discrimination, decision-making and logical conclusion. The number three, and also the colour yellow, can enhance most of the skills and faculties we associate with left-brain thinking, such as concentration, attention, deduction, problem-solving, memory and recall. Quick thought and a keen mind are common attributes of the three potential.

People who are highly influenced by the power and potential of three very often make good scientists, academicians, teachers, researchers or computer specialists, to cite some examples. They will succeed at most of the things that require acute attention to detail and a quick, active and alert mind. The challenge of new thought, pursuit of theories, evidence to the contrary or in support of and the limits of discovery often cause great excitement and interest in number three people.

The power and energy of three is a masculine potential which has similar qualities to the power and energy of one. Number threes can be active, progressive, optimistic and outgoing. Three is a number which is often associated with luck, fate and good fortune. The truth is, though, that number three people earn their own good fortune. Three is another warm, dynamic, achieving energy, used primarily for intellectual pursuit and success.

Three is an extrovert, social type of energy. People who are highly influenced by the potential of three are sometimes known for their mercurial wit. They can be lively and vivacious people who make good, stimulating company. There is a creative potential behind the number three which may be put to use in advertising, journalism, public relations and communication industries. Whereas number two people get emotionally involved with their creative callings, number threes tend to be more dispassionate and will appreciate technical precision and content, for instance, more than depth of feeling and aesthetic formation.

Relationships tend to be very important to those of us who are strongly influenced in our lives by the power and potential of three. Whereas a number one person often aims for physical attraction and sensual expression through relationships, and a number two person often aims for emotional contact and empathy through relationships, a number three person often aims for a meeting of minds. Mental aptitude and mental appreciation for life get good marks from a number three person.

Just as shades of yellow can turn to shades of gold, so too can intellect and logic turn to wisdom and to knowing, especially if the potential of three works in harmony alongside its shadow number, six. In ancient wisdom it was said that if a person travels once around the triangle he will achieve an intellectual learning; if he travels twice around the triangle he will achieve a profound wisdom and knowing. In other words, when we dig a little deeper, beyond the realms of intellect and reason, we may acquire a greater treasure and a greater sagacity and consciousness.

Challenges
Perhaps the major challenge of the three potential is to ensure that you do not rely on this power alone for knowledge, learning, growth or success. All too often people who are highly influenced by the power of three allow themselves to be limited by their intellectual, logical thinking, and thereby fail to enjoy the challenge of their much-neglected and maligned inner, instinctual and intuitive dimensions and potentials. If we are not careful the power of three can overshadow and eclipse our intuitive, feminine potentials.

by the irrational and overshadowed by ...gs, emotions, intuition and instinct. Learning, studying and academia may not come easily where there is an absence of threes. Also, the ability to apply yourself, to concentrate, focus and commit yourself, may also be a challenge to a person with no number threes.

When the power of three is imbalanced in some way or overcharged, clever becomes critical, insight turns to prejudgement, optimism gives way to doubt, enthusiasm is considered foolishness, and happiness must defend itself against cynicism. Your perception of the world can easily deteriorate if you fail to control the potential of three in your life, so much so that you can easily find yourself retreating into the 'non-risk world' of the cynic, the pessimist and the non-committed.

The power of three can also activate the ego. People influenced by the power of three can abuse their cleverness by becoming boastful, conceited and self-advertising. They never relax, and are always on the lookout to make their point. Cleverness can easily crumble. The gifts of three can easily be wasted on *Trivial Pursuit*, crosswords and other distractions. As with the power and potential of number one, number three can promote success—but what sort of success, and what will your success mean? The power of the three should never try to go it alone without its shadow number six. It will be tempted to try, though.

Because people who are highly influenced by three are usually the cerebral type, they will often conveniently forget, neglect or avoid practical tasks in life. They may, for instance, avoid the gardening or the housework, forget to do the shopping, neglect their physical health, fail to relax, and delay and procrastinate over other such practicalities. You should always remember that *the mind of you is not the whole of you.*

In relationships, the power of three is mostly attracted by the qualities of mind and of intellect in a partner or friend. Because the physical, the emotional and the spiritual are not always considered as important as mental harmony and agreement these areas may be neglected and relationships may suffer. There are, of course, exceptions to the rule, in that some number threes enjoy and appreciate opposites. They like a person to be genuine and unpretentious. They will often seek balance and harmony in themselves by relating to someone who is more intuitive, more feminine and more relaxed than they are.

The essential challenge of the power of three is to ensure that you do not neglect the University of Life! Number three people often need to learn how to let go, to play, enjoy and just 'be'. Those of us who are strongly influenced by the number three may also need to learn to break away from the secure, non-risk perch of our mental world and get stuck into life.

Feelings and emotions need to be acknowledged and expressed rather than suppressed and repressed. Instead of just clinically analysing and theorizing, try to ensure that you practise, experience and truly engage your whole self in all that you do and in all that you live through. *Mental living denies the fullness of what life has to offer.* It may be safe but it is rarely, if ever, satisfying.

Four

The power and potential of the number four is linked to the vibrations of green. Green is the predominating colour on the land of our Planet, and as such is a symbol for Earth and for earthing. ... concepts and qualities, such as foundations and strength, love and the heart, determination and will.

In sacred geometry the number four is connected with the square, an ancient symbol of the East, the Orient and North America for Earth. The square features in our common everyday language. We describe honest transactions as *fair and square*; nourishing meals are *square* meals; when we agree with someone we say that we *square* with them; equality, parity and evenness are sometimes described as *all square*; and, if we need to assert ourselves we will *square up to someone*. All of these interesting phrases and idioms give us clues as to the power and potential of number four.

Four is also associated with the four arms of the cross, again a very common Earth symbol in ancient cultures and civilizations. Both the square and the cross have also been revered as power symbols which impart inspiration, strength, determination and will. These qualities are also common potentials linked with the power of four. The power of four is a force that can move mountains.

In astrology the power and potential of four corresponds, in particular, to the signs Leo ('I will') and Scorpio ('I desire'), and also to the red Planet, Mars. In sacred anatomy the number four is connected with a subtle body of energy called the *Causal Body*, which is sometimes described as the 'body of will' and as the 'feeding body'. It is a feminine body and is activated particularly at night-time. Four is also associated with the red, base, reproduction chakra, and to the four chambers of the physical heart. Four is also linked to the day Thursday.

In the history of Creation, numerology states that after consciousness, God decided there was a need for a body of will to activate consciousness. God invoked, therefore, the power of four, revered for its building properties, for its earthing power and for its strength of will. Now, with the advent of four, the powers of one, two and three could each call upon an energy of direction and of will.

Assets

The number four empowers will, determination, endeavour and discipline. It is a working potential which can strengthen attention to detail, promote the ability to create and implement procedures and systems; it also enjoys routine. Number four people often show great persistence, faith, application and downright dogged determination in pursuit of what they desire. They can be a great asset and support to have on your side.

The number four holds invaluable potential. Its influence teaches that you have unlimited potential, and that you can liberate this unlimited potential with the help of three keys. Those of us who allow ourselves to be significantly influenced by the power and potential of the number four will find that we earn our success and our happiness through these three keys, which are work, will and persistence.

The power and potential of the number four is a building power, and as such is often put to good use in social and occupational circles. The power of four can, particularly if influenced by the shadow number five, empower a person with natural supporting qualities, with counselling and mediating skills, and also with a flair for team leadership. People who are influenced by the power of four can make good motivators. They employ a strong, feminine power to nurture, inspire, uplift and achieve, for themselves and for others.

The desire to work for others and for popular causes is a common attribute and potential of the power of four, particularly when working alongside its shadow power of five. Very often people who are significantly influenced by the powers of both four and five work, campaign and

support ecological, environ........ ....
groups and committees. They care and work passionately
for the rights, freedoms and welfare of others.

People who are highly influenced by the power and
potential of four could often be described as being *four
square*—direct, up-front, reliable and trustworthy. Number
four people aim to enjoy honest, straightforward,
no-nonsense relationships. They enjoy a strong sense of
romance, which may best be described as a practical
romance. For instance, a number four person would
probably prefer to buy a loved one a plant rather than a
rose, because the plant will last a lot longer! Honesty,
loyalty to the cause and commitment to making a relationship work are also common attributes of a number four
person.

Challenges

Almost all the challenges of number four are to do with
misguided, uncontrolled or overactivated willpower.
People who are highly influenced by the power of four
sometimes become workaholics. They are so empowered
by the need and desire to work and to achieve that they
sometimes fail or neglect to relax, release and let go. Social
life, recreation and romance may all suffer as a consequence. They may soon gain a reputation for being
sombre, dull and a bit of a 'square'. This is because they
have made the classic mistake of living to work, rather
than working to live.

The wonderful qualities of work, will and persistence,
as so often epitomized by number fours, can soon turn to
stubbornness, obstinacy and dogmatism if the power of
four is not carefully balanced and controlled. This is particularly so when there is no semblance of an attempt to
balance the qualities and potential of four with the qualities
and potential of five. A common consequence of this imbal-

ance is that the constructive qualities deteriorate into destructive ones.

Perhaps one of the most worrying aspects of a misguided, uncontrolled or overactivated power of four is a tendency to use anger, violence and force as a substitute for constructive, creative will. Frustrations, blockages and illness are a common scenario whenever the power and strength of four is abused. A tendency to be argumentative, to play continually devil's advocate, to bully and to scold are also characteristics of an overactivated, uncontrolled potential of four.

Common qualities of an underactivated number four may include manifestations of physical, emotional and/or mental weakness, carelessness, indiscipline, poor application, unreliability and an inability to concentrate. Overactivated or underactivated, a failure to control the power of four can often cause tiredness, exhaustion and excessive depletion. For this reason many ancient civilizations would meditate and pray to a cross or a square for renewed strength.

Having no number fours in one's numerology chart can create a number of interesting challenges. Without a number four the power of will can wilt and wane, and is often left wanting. The ability to support yourself and others can also be a challenge to a chart with no number fours. Dedication, direction and determination depend to a large extent upon the potential of four, although it can also be found in the potential of other numbers. The ability to work well for what you want will also be a dynamic challenge where there is either an absence of four or an untapped potential of four.

Above all, the major challenge facing a number four person is how best to use his or her extraordinary powers of will, not only for him- or herself but for the good of family, friends, the community and the world. Once again, this involves a serious and careful appreciation and attunement to the potential and power of the shadow number five. Paradoxically enough, *selflessness can empower personal will; sustained selfishness can sink it.*

Five

The Taoists of China, the Indians of North America and the Yogis of Tibet are just a few of the many varied cultures that have revered the number five as a power of Nature. They saw it as an expression of the *vital, universal life-force* which sustains, connects and interweaves throughout all Creation. Each culture witnessed the power of Five in evidence all around them. They found it, for example, in the five elements (wood, water, fire, air, ether), in the five fingers and five toes of the human body, in the five main internal organs of the body, and in the five petals of a rose and many other similar botanical forms. Five was therefore connected with life-force and also fertility.

The power of five was also revered by these same cultures as a 'doorway to the collective' and as the 'gate of heaven'. Five continues to be considered a collective power which drives, supports and furthers the evolution of all of the worlds. While the power of four is thought to provide a similar potential to that of five, it does so only on an individual basis. The power of five performs functions similar to those of the power of four, but does so on a collective basis, and thus, being essentially collective by nature, it is considered a superior power to that of four.

In many ways the numbers four and five represent for numerology the fulcrum point of life and of Creation. The numbers one to four represent, for example, the journey from spirit into matter; the numbers five to nine represent the return journey home from matter to spirit. Also, the numbers one to four represent the birth of individual consciousness and personal will, physical survival and material success; the numbers five to nine represent the evolution of collective consciousness, group will, human survival and spiritual success.

The differences between the number four and the number five are again clearly illustrated in the art of sacred anatomy, where the number four is associated with the *physical heart* and the number five with the thymus area, which is often described as the *spiritual heart*, or *collective heart*. The physical heart is the doorway to the life of yourself; the spiritual heart is the doorway to the life of humanity.

In geometry, the number five is joined with the five-pointed star, or Star of David, its five rays reaching out and embracing all life. The five-pointed star is also thought to symbolize the human form, and thereby natural man. In astrology the number five is linked with, in particular, the sign Libra ('I balance') and the Planet Saturn. Five is also associated with Friday.

In the history of Creation, numerology described a sequence of events whereby after God, the Creator, had invoked the power of individual, human will, through the potential of four, God decided it was then necessary for humanity to have a link with the greater collective, universal and omniscient Will of Creation. This link was provided by the power and potential of the number five.

Assets

The power and potential of the number five can promote astonishing versatility, so much so that people who allow themselves to be strongly influenced by the number five can turn their hands to almost anything. Number five people are often quick in thought, unconventional and progressive. They often relish change, adapt easily, and seek variety actively. Nothing has to be the way it is, and nothing should stay the same for long. They may also see the world as their oyster. Other people see them as being 'naturally-gifted'.

The number five tends to promote a desire to travel, a need to taste adventure, and an ambition to learn and to know how others live.

The number five encourages you to look out for alternative angles, for fresh perspectives and new horizons. Those of us who allow ourselves to be influenced by the power and potential of five often feel and believe we are *world citizens*.

The personal creative potential of the number five can be very pure. Number fives often realize their own natural creative capacities. Their art may sometimes be shocking, and will always set out to make us think about, see and explore fresh fields and new horizons. As well as the creative attributes, the power of five also advances the need and desire to communicate. Therefore, the power of five often influences journalists, correspondents, writers, artists, musicians, advertising executives, public relations consultants and teachers, for example, all of whom create and convey messages.

The power of five, when evident, is often experienced by others as charisma and magnetism. Number five people are sometimes 'larger than life' characters. They can be magnanimous, generous, kind, loving, and are very often well thought of. Those of us who allow ourselves to be influenced by the collective powers of five may sometimes aim for careers where we can be seen regularly in the public eye.

The potential of five often helps a person to put things into perspective. This is vital as a means of combating stress, anxiety, neuroses and other mental illnesses which are often experienced during times of pressure or hardship. It is also interesting to note that number five people often describe themselves as a *channel*—a channel for creativity, communication and healing, perhaps.

Challenges

The challenges of five centre around the moral and ethical use of their considerable talents. A volatile, uncontrolled use of the power of five can tear a person down as quickly as a well-controlled use can build a person up. Number five people can naturally find it easy to gain confidence in people. This, too, they can abuse, and thereby be deceitful, dishonest, deceptive, illusive and misguiding. They can glide with a glib tongue, and are often renowned as confidence tricksters.

The appreciation of variety can become an insurmountable need for variety if the power of five is not properly earthed. As a result, number fives can often be found to be constantly changing addresses, occupations and relationships. The ability to commit to a single cause is often lacking, most probably because of a weakness for temptations and low boredom thresholds. Here, then, is a good illustration that, although five may be higher than four on the numerological ladder, it still needs the qualities of four, such as earthing, commitment and loyalty, to bring out the best in itself.

Misuse and poor control of the five potential can mean that we easily dissipate our skills and talents if they are not carefully focused. We can end up being a jack of all trades but master of none. This will be frustrating to those of us who are significantly influenced by the power of five, because we will possess an inner feeling and knowing that we are really capable of a lot more. Once again, the power of five needs the power of four for persistence, discipline and sustained endeavour.

The power of five offers you the potential to dig deep within yourself and to manifest, thereby, a greater potential than you may think or dream you are capable of. The challenge of five is to not give up digging too soon, and also to not dilly-dally on the surface of things for too long. Popularity, charisma, fame and fortune may prevent you from attaining even greater things. You will know if this is true to you if you harbour a feeling of being unhappy with what you have achieved so far. You may have to sacrifice image for substance, glamour for meaning. Success, talents and ambitions need to be carefully managed.

Having no number fives in a full numerology chart, or having an untapped potential of five, can test the fullness of your life. Five is a key that opens up the collective realms of potential within you. Without a manifested five potential you may have to look to the potentials of other numbers to acquire collective belonging, brotherhood, cosmic inspiration, wisdom, spiritual love and unconditional service. When five is not alive, a person must make sure to challenge him- or herself to contribute to and live not only for themselves, but for the whole of the human race. *Five is for family—the family of humanity*.

Six

The power of six can be obtained by doubling the power of three. The powers of six and of three have, therefore, certain similar potentials that centre on and around knowledge, reason and intellect. It is one of the fundamental tenets of numerological lore that when a number is doubled to form a new number, that new number is a complete transformation of the old number. It takes on twice as much power, and much, much more. Thus, the potential of six stands not only for knowledge, reason and intellect, but also for profound and rare qualities of insight, wisdom and knowing.

In astrology the number six is sometimes linked especially to the Planet Mercury and also to the signs Gemini ('I think'), Sagittarius ('I see') and Aquarius ('I know'). In sacred geometry the number six is associated with the interlaced triangles: one upward-pointing triangle overlapping one downward-pointing triangle. This symbol is often connected to the heart and to wisdom, and has been used, particularly in ancient Asia, as a device for contemplation, meditation and the achievement of higher states of awareness and consciousness.

In sacred anatomy the number six is associated with the solar plexus chakra, or *Seat of Learning*, with the brow chakra, or *Seat of Wisdom*, and with the throat chakra, the highest function of which is the *Communication of Wisdom*. And in alchemy, the number six is linked to the colour violet, itself a symbol for the brow chakra, and also to the colour gold, which alchemists believed to be a symbol for the highest fruits of wisdom and knowing.

In the history of Creation, numerology states that God imparted God's wisdom throughout the solar systems, throughout the Galaxies, and throughout the Universes. To perform this mighty act, God invoked the power of six. Whereas the power of three was invoked by God to help us recognize the 'how' of something, the power of six was invoked by God to help us achieve the 'why' of something. The number is indeed a symbol for a pure and profound potential.

Assets

The number six inspires wisdom, philosophy, understanding and ideals. In particular, the number six promotes the pursuit and romance of wisdom and of all things wise.

People influenced by the power of six are exceptionally appreciative. They are the gourmets of life, greatly influenced by the arts, beauty, peace and ideals. Their appetites are insatiable.

The power of six often moulds advisers, guardians, arbitrators, mediators, mentors and consultants. Number six people often are adept at 'reading between the lines', and have an acute and well-developed intuitive, *sixth sense*. Unlike number threes, people who are well influenced by the power of six are not afraid of intuition, instinct, imagination and creative conjecture. On the contrary, they are quite taken with them. True wisdom embraces both masculine and feminine. It leaves nothing out.

The power of six has creative potential. Very often, people who design for a living, be it clothes, buildings, books, etc., allow themselves to be influenced by the power of six. Number six people may also be directors, editors or producers, who guide and inspire creative operations from the helm. The strategies and challenges of management often appeal to these 'chess players'. People who allow themselves to be influenced by the power of six attract theologies, philosophies, psychologies, ideals and strategies like a magnet.

Correct procedure is vital to number sixes. Aesthetics, principles, morals and ethics are all essential. And nowhere is this more evident than in relationships. A meeting of minds is essential for long-term relationships. Mental, philosophical and spiritual companionship is valued more so perhaps than physical union and intimacy. Relationships often enjoy depth, inspire creativity, promote freedom, and must, most definitely, have both meaning and purpose.

Meaning is essential to number six people. Everything must have a meaning, be it a relationship, a career, a holiday or even a day off work. Number six people are often inspired by the idea that there is a purpose to all things.

Their favourite hobby and pursuit is to track down what exactly the purpose is. Meaning and purpose nourish and feed the soul. To a number six person, feeding the soul comes before feeding the stomach.

The power and potential of the number six can inspire the communicator in you. What you communicate about and whom you communicate to is also very important to you. On the whole, number six people are very selective in their approach to life. Making the right selection, at the right time, place and for the right reasons can be, to the number six person, what life is all about.

Challenges
The power of six can, if not carefully balanced and controlled, promote one of the most dangerous behaviours of all: idealism. Idealism can make number sixes unbearably difficult to live with at times. Idealism may feed your dreams, but it can also fuel bitter disappointment. Idealism can leave you susceptible to blind love, obsession, possessiveness and jealousy. The reverse of this is that people influenced by six can also often appear detached, aloof and difficult to approach. Partners often feel the unspoken pressure of having to live up to the standards set for them by their number six partners.

The appreciation of aesthetics can become an obsession and neurosis for those of us who operate with a poorly balanced power of six. We can be quarrelsome, objectionable, judgemental, complaining and narrow-minded, as we become dominated by a relentless and at times pointless pursuit of perfection. Frequent mental anxiety, fluctuating feelings and emotional volatility are common accompanying symptoms of this imbalance.

Having no number sixes or a poorly manifested six potential in a full numerology chart can create a number of interesting imbalances and challenges. Without the six potential you will find it very difficult to ascend the higher reaches of the mind. An appreciation of wisdom, beauty, romance and ideals, in all their finest aspects, may perhaps never be contemplated or sought for. Without the number six it is difficult to turn clever into wise, understanding into knowing, or appreciation into wonder. An absence of six can be the difference between a life that is lived and a life that is learned.

The failure to earth yourself well is a common complaint caused by a poorly balanced and controlled number six. It is often the case that a number six person can neglect the physical, the emotional and the practical in pursuit of wisdom. Number sixes may also reach for wisdom but not reason, philosophy but not logic, intuition but not intellect. This leads to a lop-sided development, in which case the quality of your wisdom must be called into question.

Another common challenge for those of us who are influenced by the power of six is not to take on too much. We can, if we are not careful, easily be susceptible to stress, exhaustion, anxiety and tension, feeling all *at sixes and sevens*. This is partly because we may be operating with a pure, collective power which so empowers us that we can easily feel as if we were a small car running on a big engine. If not careful we can easily run away with ourselves.

Those of us who are highly influenced by the power of six must not forget the people who are close to us in our life. So often we become so preoccupied with our contemplations and our meditations that we give more time to ideas and ideals than we do to the people who are attempting to share their lives with us. Human life must take priority, and should neither be overshadowed or eclipsed by dreamy ideals.

Seven

The power and potential of the number seven is often linked to the vibrations of blue, a cool, calm, reflective colour, all-pervasive and with many tones and shades ranging from deep dark sea blues to clear light sky blues. Like the colour blue, the number seven is described as a power of tranquillity, meditation and contemplation. Profundity, depth and vision are also associated with the power and potential of seven.

The philosophical schools of the Pythagorians and the Rosicrucians interpreted the potential of seven as *Spiritual Love*, or to put it another way, *Unconditional Love*. For centuries and centuries we have as a race tried to get to grips with what this word, *Love*, really means. The Pythagorians believed the answers to this age-old quest can come in meditation upon the number seven. Seven is also linked sometimes to the colours rose and pink, both of which have been described as *The Breath of God* and as symbols of *Universal Love*.

Oriental and Asian numerology systems have sometimes given the number seven another meaning. The ancient numerologists at times saw the power of seven as a collective, all-embracing potential. They therefore connected the power of seven with Brotherhood, Community, Oneness, and also *Cosmic Consciousness*, which describes a poetic, mystic ability to tune in to and be at one with all life. It is interesting to note that in some schools of alchemy the power of seven has been described as the *Power of Fusion*.

In geometry the seven is sometimes linked to the symbol of a triangle within a square. One interpretation of this symbol is the realization of balance and harmony of mind and of spirit (the triangle) in matter (the square). Another interpretation is that of the manifestation of heaven (the triangle) on Earth (the square). In geometry, therefore, the power of seven has a definite spiritual quality.

In astrology the power of seven has many associations with Planets and signs. In particular it is linked to the signs Aquarius ('I know') and Sagittarius ('I see'), and also to the Planet of Law and of Justice, Saturn. In sacred anatomy the number seven is linked to the throat chakra, described as the *Communicator of Wisdom*, and also as the *Communicator of Love*.

In the history of Creation, numerology states that after God had invoked, in particular, the powers of two (feeling), five (Collective Consciousness) and six (Wisdom), it was now necessary to activate a universal energy of connectedness, of unity and of preservation. To do so, God invoked the power of Love by radiating the power of seven.

Assets
The power of seven inspires thinkers, philosophers, psychologists and contemplatives. It also often sparks the researcher. Seven is a vibration for contemplation, meditation and deep thought. It is also a vibration of communication, particularly the communication of contemplations, truths, wisdom, and also issues of a collective, environmental or social nature. Seven can also often inspire the teacher in you.

The power of seven activates the land of spiritual dimensions within you. Spiritual reality and spiritual truth are all important to those of us who allow ourselves to be influenced significantly by the power of seven. Monks, nuns, priests, theologians and mystics are often motivated by the seven potential. The power of seven is by no means exclusive, though, to these groups alone. Very often the power of seven is just as busy in an office block, family home or cricket pitch as it is in an ashram, church or temple.

The number seven encourages service. People who allow themselves to be influenced by the power of seven are often driven by a need to make a difference in the world. They want to leave the world a better place than they found it. Therefore, social causes, the peace movements, environmental campaigns and religious organizations are often filled with number seven people.

Inventors, entrepreneurs, salespeople, marketing consultants, advertising executives, and agents of various sorts who are motivated as much by quality of service as of quality of bank account are also often influenced by the seven vibration. Quality of life and quality of service are very important to number seven people, often because spiritual rewards and spiritual satisfaction are valued above material gain.

The power of seven can promote strongly individualistic characters who are often introverts at heart and quite eccentric by nature. They are loners, comfortable with their own space for long periods of time. The need for regular retreat away from the hustle and bustle of modern life is very important. Personal freedom and an expression of independence is also very important to those of us who are profoundly influenced by the power of seven.

The seven vibration often inspires ethics, a code of conduct, dignity and chivalry within you. The spirit of romance is also part of the potential of seven—high, grand, adventurous romance rather than the soppy, weepy, emotional stuff. Unconditional love, an appreciation for other's personal space, freedom, loyalty, fidelity and integrity are all common characteristics that can be aroused by the number seven.

Challenges

Those of us who are influenced by the seven potential can, if we are not careful, see the world through rose-coloured spectacles. The reality we see is not always the reality we might wish for. There is a tendency, therefore, to retreat and live in a Walter Mitty world of dreams, wishes and illusions. Escapism, procrastination, rationalization, displacement, denial and a general inability to cope with life, particularly with practicalities, is common.

Instead of being a loner for healthy reasons, number sevens can easily become loners for all the wrong reasons. Facing up to emotions and also to physical survival may be too difficult. We may end up, therefore, wearing emotional armour which leaves us protected but also completely indifferent to and detached from people, feelings and emotions. Independence and freedom can soon become isolation and loneliness if we are not careful.

Failure to invest in the spiritual somewhere along the line can leave those of us who are influenced by the number seven feeling empty, dissatisfied and devoid of inner happiness. Furthermore, the reach towards spiritual satisfaction can, unfortunately, give way to more earthy gratifications, found, for instance, in drink, drugs and promiscuity.

This failure to invest in and focus upon the spiritual can be caused by an absence of the number seven in a full numerology chart. Seven is the key to mystical, spiritual and unconditional love. One of the challenges of having no or only poorly manifested sevens is, therefore, to look to the potentials of other numbers to feed and support the experiences and lessons of universal, creative love. Without seven it can be very challenging indeed to even consider a quest for peace, love and service. Without the seven potential physical emotions can eclipse pure, philosophical love.

To activate and work with the power of seven is a lifetime challenge. Very often we will decide, therefore, to forgo the challenge this time around and fall back upon the shadow power of two. It appears altogether more easy to work with the number two; seven goes a bit too deep. However, if we fail to balance the powers of two and seven we can easily lay ourselves open to emotional turbulence. Just as a still, clear blue sea is one of the most peaceful and powerful of Nature's wonders, so, also, is a deep, turbulent sea one of Nature's most destructive and terrifying forces.

With imbalance, neglect and blockages the potential of seven can turn unconditional attributes into judge-mental, critical behaviours. Independence and freedom may become selfish, irresponsible self-indulgence; emo-tional faith can disintegrate into emotional insecurity; and possessiveness and obsessiveness can proliferate in place of moderation, generosity and magnanimous measures.

The route to the potential of seven is an inner one. Facing up to oneself, the search for self-knowledge and the drive towards self-discovery and growth of the soul should not be relegated from reality to dreams, for this very often is when problems begin for those of us who do not allow ourselves to face up to the potential of seven. When you attend to the seven, you attend to your own inner patch.

Eight

The power and potential of number eight is often linked to the colour magenta (a mix of blues and reds), renowned for its leadership, communication and organizational qua-lities, and also to the colour indigo, renowned for its artistic and creative flair. Both magenta and indigo are also colours associated with healers and medicos, and also with psychics and visionaries.

In sacred anatomy the number eight is associated with the indigo brow chakra, known as the *Centre of Psychic Sight* and the *Centre of Psychic Control*. The potential of eight is closely linked to profound feminine intuition and insight. Number eight people often have an intuitive feel for what they do, and are often described by others as 'naturals'. Success would appear to come easily and effortlessly to number eights.

Eight is also connected with the orange hara, or abdomen chakra, *Centre of Digestion*—physical, mental, emotional and spiritual digestion. Eight is therefore a number linked to the mental churnings and machinations of the deep unconscious mind. It is also a number with many golden and gifted qualities. In astrology the number eight has associations in particular with the Sun and with Jupiter, Planet of the arts, and also with the signs Sagittarius ('I see') and Capricorn ('I use').

Ancient numerologists have sometimes interpreted the potential of eight as that Energy which networks, circuits, connects and organizes the worlds. Eight represents the point at which the infinite and finite merge, where the spiritual materializes and matter spiritualizes, where the implicate and explicate exchange, where the introvert and extrovert meet, where the esoteric and exoteric change over, where the unconscious becomes conscious and vice versa, and also where life follows death and death follows life.

In geometry the number eight is drawn up and down the staff of the caduceus symbol (two snakes entwined around a rod or staff). This symbol is thought to represent the circuits and cycles that support and perpetuate life. Eight is also sometimes represented as the double cross or the double square. This is partly because eight can be obtained by doubling the power of four. Thus, the power of eight has close affinities to the potential of four and also to the potential of the shadow number one, both of which promote action, endeavour and will. Eight embraces these influences, but, curiously enough, also embraces more subtle qualities of inaction, tolerance, permission and channelling. We can use the potential of eight to tune in to thoughts, ideas and actions that filter through or bubble up from our unconscious, intuitive realms.

In the history of Creation, numerology states that God, the Creator, invoked the power of eight to create a circuit, or framework upon which all of God's Creation could be supported, connected and made to evolve. It is through the power of eight that Spirit dissolves into matter and matter can be transmuted into Spirit. Eight is the spiral, the stairway and the spiritual DNA that leads from Heaven to Earth and back again.

Assets

Eight inspires energy, dynamism, endeavour and pursuit. Those of us who allow ourselves to be influenced by the power and potential of eight are often naturally successful at what we do, though it is often the case that we do not necessarily invest as much importance in our own success as others around us might. The quest for new horizons and the power of eternal hope are often promoted through the potential of the number eight.

Management, organization, planning, administration, personnel work, control and authority often rest well with those of us who are influenced significantly by the power of eight. If the number eight and the number one are carefully balanced, the influence of eight promotes solid, down-to-earth, sturdy, supportive and consistent quali-ties. Another quality of this union will be the thoughtful and perceptive setting and achieving of goals.

Unlike the aim of the number one, the aim of eight is not necessarily material success and wealth. On the contrary, self-development, inner values, philosophical aims, ethical standards, the growth of the soul, spiritual realization and internal gratification are often the aims. Number eight people are often very successful at what they do, and may well enjoy material success and wealth as a result. These gains are rarely the motivating factors, however, for a number eight person.

Being supportive, particularly to groups and in love, marriage, home and friendship, is a trademark of the eight potential. Eight people feel a need to be connected to and a part of things. Indeed, they thrive on it. Being a loner does not appeal to the potential of eight. Thus, number eight people often make themselves available to others. They are people whom others can depend upon, turn to for strength and look to for a plan of action or a method of support.

The power of eight promotes creativity and intuition. Like the colours magenta and indigo, the power of eight activates the qualities of right-brain thought. A holistic outlook, unique creative expression, high imagination and intuitive knowing are qualities inspired by the power of eight. An ambition for creativity and spiritual truth and values are also common qualities.

Psychic skills and abilities are also a typical feature of the potential of eight. Clairvoyance, clairsentience, psychometry, mediumship and other psychic phenomena may manifest through and around the appearance of eight. Very often, however, the shadow number one, a particularly physical and material power, may prevent and deny psychic opening.

Healing is another common quality of the eight potential. Those of us who allow ourselves to open up to the power of eight may find we are natural healers. We may work in the healing and health professions, such as counselling, complementary medicines, psychology, surgery, medicine or nursing. Or, we may be unofficial, unpaid agony aunts and uncles who naturally attract people who feel we may be able to help.

Challenges

Eight appears to promote apparently 'natural' talents and skills easily, effortlessly and automatically. A common challenge of eight is, therefore, to remain continually open to your innate potential. Watch out for, allow, turn inwards, realize, give permission to and feed your inner self so that the influence of eight is not blocked. Eight uses a person as a channel. Success does not so much come *from* you as *through* you.

Eight is a challenging number, full of personal surprises. It is an energy that you flow with rather than attempt to confine or control. This experience can make you feel uncomfortable, so much so that you can easily opt to fall back on the shadow number one, and thereby the intuitive, the imaginative, the creative and the spiritual are all ignored.

There is safety here but not satisfaction. The eight and the one must work together and not in isolation, just as the numbers seven and two, six and three, and five and four must do so. Of course the real truth is that no number can afford to exist on its own. This is one of the lessons and challenges of the eight potential.

Eight has a peculiar relationship to death. Many people leave the physical world during a number eight year or during a number eight cycle. This is why eight is sometimes associated with bad luck. Eight does not, however, deal only with physical death. It is also about emotional, mental and spiritual death, and about birth and rebirth. Many number eight people work with the elderly and work with death on a daily basis.

One of the key challenges of number eight is not to 'die' to the potential of eight. Tune in to your intuitive self, contact your creative self, allow the inner teacher to talk and give permission for your psychic self to open. So often the potential of one eclipses the potential of eight, so much so that it is possible to live your entire life without ever experiencing the potential of eight in action.

Driving yourself and others too hard, an obsession with finances and wealth, exhaustion and fatigue, trying to go it alone and a failure to delegate well are also common characteristics of a poorly controlled power of eight. Eight is another collective potential. It is easy to let its energy run away with you. If you are influenced significantly by the eight potential you may find it beneficial to pace yourself, to relax and centre yourself on a regular basis.

Having no number eights in a full numerology chart can create gaps and spaces in your life that may amount to tangible tests and concrete challenges. For instance, without eight you rely upon other numbers to network, circuit, connect and organize your life. You may experience, therefore, an innate, free-floating sense of isolation and not-belonging. Spiritual sunlight may for a long time be clouded over by a preoccupation with the physical. Without the eight influence you may also not consider yourself connected to God, to the Creator and to the Absolute, but this does not mean to say that the connections are not there.

If you rely too much on the shadow power of one instead of balancing the one with the eight, many of the challenges of one will apply to your life. A central challenge has to do with success. Success often comes easily to those of us who are influenced by one and by eight. But what quality of success? Sometimes, if we are not careful, we become much more interested in the 'trappings' of success than in what the success means and at what we have been successful. Remember your potential is limitless, and remember also that material ambition and success die quick deaths. Good advice would be to aim higher, dig deeper and take a wider view, and also to seek, invest in and attend to the world within you as much as the world around you.

Nine

The power and potential of the number nine is linked to the powers of Law, completion and balance. It is therefore often associated with the colour white and also with the colour relationship between white, black and grey. The powers of assessment, discrimination and judgement, which help a person distinguish clearly between black and white, are also linked to the power and potential of the number nine.

The nine potential is also commonly connected to the violet vibration. Both the number nine and the colour violet promote creativity and stimulate right-brain functions such as imagination, intuition and holistic perception. Nine liberates the inner artist in you. It also stirs your natural, innate healing potential. If you allow yourself to awaken the power of nine within you, you can also stimulate and stir your psychic self.

In geometry the power of the number nine is linked to the power of three triangles, which is a common symbol for completion and perfection. We mentioned earlier the ancient law which states that to travel around the triangle once you become knowledge and to travel around the triangle twice you become wisdom—the completion of this law states that to travel around the triangle thrice you become Law.

In astrology the nine potential is associated in particular with the signs Sagittarius ('I see') and Pisces ('I believe'), and also with Saturn, *Seat of Karmic Justice*. And in sacred anatomy, the number nine is linked to the violet brow chakra, which is the *Third Eye*, or *Seat of Pure Sight*. The brow chakra is commonly associated with insight, objectivity, values, truth and discrimination.

In the history of Creation, numerology states that God, the Creator, invoked the power of nine, and thereby finished the initial Work. Nine represents completion, perfection and the end of a cycle. There now existed, therefore, a cycle and a stairway which could project from God to Spirit into matter, and also from Spirit out of matter back to God again. With the advent of nine, the full course for the journey of involution and evolution had now been set.

Assets
The power and potential of the number nine activates the watching mechanism in you. Little or nothing escapes your attention. Your perception is crystal clear, and your discrimination razor sharp. You are motivated by truth, fairness and justice. It is not uncommon, therefore, for lawyers, solicitors, judges, magistrates, detectives, scientists, overseers, supervisors, researchers and member of other similar professionals to be empowered by the nine potential.

The number nine promotes intuitive truth, diagnosis and judgement. People who allow themselves to open up to the power of nine often act on inner hunches and unconscious promptings. Number nine people are often renowned for their fair- and broad-mindedness. They are generous people who believe in the innate integrity of others; they are often prepared to give people the benefit of the doubt. In other words, they place great emphasis on the giving of trust, on being trusted and on acting in a trustworthy manner.

Number nine feeds dignity, honour and an awareness of the important responsibility of setting an example for others. The power of nine also instils a sense of duty and service to others. Indeed, service, sacrifice and selflessness, sometimes to an astonishing degree, are common hallmarks of number nine people. Many people in positions of power and authority are influenced strongly by the power of nine somewhere in their numerology chart.

Creative expression is another hallmark of the number nine potential. Because of the skills of objective measurement and impartial assessment associated with nine, number nine people often make good critics, editors, directors, producers and trainers in the arts. Otherwise, number nine people are often patrons of the arts to a high degree.

The nine potential is often interpreted as a healing vibration. Spiritual and psychic healers are often influenced by the power of nine. Sometimes the healing power is not so obvious, but it is still there. People may feel good around a number nine person without necessarily knowing why. Professionals in healing and in medicine, such as doctors, nurses, etc., but also forensic scientists, medical researchers and laboratory technicians and assistants, are often significantly influenced by the power of nine.

Nine supports psychic development. Some of the most extraordinary healers, mediums, psychics and visionaries have been those who have allowed themselves to open up to the power of nine. Each of us has an intuitive, psychic and creative nature. Whether you recognize this or not, and whether you choose to work with this nature constructively or not, depends by and large on the quality of your relationship to the power of nine. The question is, *will you own or reject your power of nine?*

Challenges

Those of us who are influenced significantly by the power of nine must make sure that we resist the temptation to become a law unto ourselves. Nine attracts power. We have a choice, as always, to use the power wisely or foolishly. Very often, if we are not wise, we will act irresponsibly and shall abuse such power. When influenced by the power of nine you must attempt to remain uncorrupted. Truth and integrity must be your guiding lights.

The power of nine promotes qualities of intuition, judgement and discrimination. There is, unfortunately, no guarantee that your intuition, judgement and discrimination shall necessarily always be accurate. As previously stated, the power of nine activates the watching mechanism within you. This watching mechanism can become clouded, dirty and poorly focused if you do not continually attune, polish and care for it. You must not make the mistake, therefore, of thinking that your judgements are always beyond reproach.

Nine can promote great stability. On the other hand, it also can sprinkle seeds of great instability. Number nines must be careful that they do not become renowned for being a *nine days' wonder*: clever, sensational and scintillating one moment, disappointing, unimpressive and inconsistent the next. Ups and downs, highs and lows, peaks and troughs are often part of the experience of a poorly controlled nine potential, one minute being on *cloud nine*, the next minute feeling *nine foot under*. The number nine potential can take you all the way to the top. But what is the top? And how long can you stay there?

Having no number nines in a full numerology chart, or

having a neglected nine potential, can spark challenges and tests galore. Lacking a number nine, a person must work well with other numbers to develop a relationship with law, truth and wisdom. The potentials of three and six in particular rely very much on the bright Planet of nine for direction, safety, objectivity and guidance. Nine is a symbol for *Higher Self*. With no nines, or with underactivated nines, it is easy to neglect your full, innate potential. The challenge of nine is always to open up to the wisdom of higher potential and *Higher Self*.

Creative, holistic and broad-minded expression can easily deteriorate into petty jealousy, selfishness, constant self-opinionating and narrow-mindedness if you overactivate nine's judgement mechanism. The constructive critic becomes a damaging one, devoid of any artistic talent of his or her own. The pursuit of perfectionism can become both perverted and painful, for yourself and for others, if you are not balanced and careful.

In relationships, an uncontrolled power of nine can lead to a temptation to dominate, swamp and control others. Impossible standards, rules, criticism, jealousy and obsession may proliferate. On the other hand, an unbalanced power of nine may also promote disinterest, detachment and no standards at all. The potential of nine may promote either the most conscientious or unconscientious behaviour. As always in numerology, the difference comes with how you use the potential.

Many number nine people can often seem quite eccentric to others. They lead seemingly irregular lifestyles, strive for independence, and inevitably leave their unique mark. They are individuals, and will often go out of their way to demonstrate this fact. The power of nine often promotes larger-than-life characters. To the number nine person, life is like a field of great big fruit trees. The fruits are there for the taking, but sometimes the fruits are too exotic and too gorgeous to know where to begin.

Honest self-judgement and fair self-evaluation are key challenges associated with the number nine power. These challenges apply to all of us. The ability to know oneself is the key to self-control, self-kindness and self-realization. Knowledge liberates potential. Positive self-evaluation is a definite help; negative self-evaluation a definite deterrent. The ability to centre continually, to self-analyse in an objective and fair manner, to know how to care and look after yourself, are all important qualities you may learn to master if you are significantly influenced by the power of nine in your life.

Zero

The zero is more of a nothing than a number. There are no personal birthdate numbers or personal name numbers, for instance, that are zero. There is not a year, month, day or minute that is a zero time. And yet the zero, or 'the nothing', has a definite, calculable affect on the numbers, dates and times of numerology.

In geometry the zero, or 'the nothing' is associated with the circle. Both the zero and the circle are symbols of fullness, wholeness, *roundedness* and completion. Paradoxically, the zero and the circle are also symbols of emptiness, nothingness and non-existence. The zero and the circle are also symbols of both the time before the beginning and the time after the end.

In the history of Creation, numerology states that God, the Creator, had to 'start from zero'. Zero represents the stage on which all the mythologies of Creation are set. The *Void*, the *primordial waters*, the *nothingness*, the *that which is not*, the *time before time*, and also, paradoxically, the *end after the end* are all wrapped up in the zero.

Zero is not really associated with colour. Instead it is linked to opaqueness and also to transparency and to translucency. Zero is linked to the *Cosmic Mirror*. Thus, whenever the zero appears it is an excellent time to hold a mirror up to yourself for self-examination and -discovery. Zero is also connected with clarity, unobstructed vision, and the transmission of light and lucidity.

Zero is also linked to another concept, namely the *Cosmic Lens*. Thus, during the tenth day of each month it is good to analyse the action of the number one in your life. During the twentieth day of each month it is good to analyse the effects of the number two in your life. And during the thirtieth day of each month it is good to analyse the action of the number three in your life. If a zero appears in your personal birthdate number then it is good to cultivate the skill of regularly looking into your life, with as much clarity and lucidity as possible.

In sacred anatomy the zero is linked to the space beneath and the space below the physical body. It is thus a symbol for all of the space that is beyond you. Zero is also associated with the soul, and in particular with its purity. In Chinese philosophy this purity is described as the *uncarved block* which is not yet soiled or dirtied by the experience of life. Zero persuades you to do some soul-searching, to identify your original conception and to contact that space within you which is beyond space and time.

Zero stands for both the unmanifest potential and the finished work. During the time of ten, look for the unmanifest potential and the finished work of the number one. What is the full, unmanifest potential of number one? What is the completeness, the fullness of number one? You may like to do this exercise with each of the nine primary integers. It is designed to help you explore and go beyond yourself.

If you look into the zero it is as if you are looking into the entrance or exit of a long channel or tube. Whenever a zero appears in your life it represents an opportunity for you to become a channel for thoughts, expressions and ideas. It is a time to be effortless, motionless, open and peaceful, like the unruffled surface of a clear, still pond. Wait and watch for what might come. The potential of the Universe might choose you to express itself through you.

CHAPTER THREE

YOUR PERSONAL BIRTHDATE NUMBER

Your *personal birthdate number* is derived from the arrangement of numbers which make up your date of birth. This number is probably the most significant and influential number in your life. It represents the potentials, possibilities and probabilities you have chosen to work with and manifest here on Earth.

The quality of your relationship with your personal birthdate number can determine and reflect the quality of your relationship with life. This relationship can often serve as a platform for your greatest strengths and successes in life. Great care must be taken, therefore, to ensure that this platform is both solid and secure, for you may well depend upon its power for self-growth, self-expression and self-realization.

You are the custodian of your personal birthdate number. You are not ruled by this number, or at least you should not be. Numbers are your tools. They are your servants, not your masters. They represent the potential which is yours to explore, discover, play and express yourself with. You own your numbers; your numbers do not own you.

Your personal birthdate number is a very significant signpost which may well point to the direction, purpose and meaning of your life. It very often signals your motivations, ambitions, values and very own *raison d'être*. Therefore it can be very useful to turn to numbers when you need guidance or direction, or if you must make a decision. Self-counselling by numbers can be a very powerful therapy.

Working with numbers can help you open up to and create new possibilities in your life. And one of the highest truths of the philosophy of numbers is that *you are surrounded by all possibilities*. A conscious, day-to-day relationship with numbers can serve as a reminder to you of your innate potential to be able to cope and deal with what you undertake or are presented with in life.

The Formula

In the East and the Orient, such was the importance of the personal birthdate number that, in some of the ancient mystery schools, its formula was kept a closely guarded secret, made available only to a chosen few through a ritual of initiation. In other ancient schools the formula was revealed more freely. For instance, a person would very often receive his or her personal birthdate number as a coming-of-age gift. Great dignity would be attached to the value and meaning of this number, and a person would guard its sanctity with all his or her honour.

In the West, the science of heraldry, medals and family crests has also been influenced by the science and philosophy of numbers, though it is true today that on the great majority of modern cloths little or no significance is given to numbers. However, in previous centuries a person's personal birthdate number was his or her signature in life, and was carried about as a reminder of potential and destiny. Once again, great pride and dignity was vested in this number.

To arrive at your personal birthdate number, take the number of the day of your birth, the number of the month of your birth, and the number of your year of birth, and then add them all together. As an example we shall take the date of birth of Walt Disney, the American pioneer of cartoon films: 5th December 1901.

Birth day	+	Birth month	+	Year of birth	=	Personal Number

Birth day   =   5
Birth month   =   3   (12: 1 + 2 = 3)
Year of birth   =   2   (1 + 9 + 0 + 1 = 11: 1 + 1 = 2)
Personal Number =   **1**   (5 + 3 + 2 = 10: 1 + 0 = 1)

Walt Disney's personal birthdate number is the number one. It is highly likely, therefore, that the power of one would have been both a motivating force and possible potential in Walt Disney's life. The 'original', the 'pioneer', the 'leader' and the 'entrepreneur' are all potentials that are often inspired by the number one power. It would appear that Walt Disney made good use of this potential in his life.

The number one potential would not have been the only numerological influence in Walt Disney's life, for no person is influenced by one number alone. Indeed, the highest truth of numerology is that *we are all numbers*. It is true to say, however, that the power and potential of your personal birthdate number is very often the predominating force in your life. Whether or not you choose to work with this potential is, of course, up to you. The choice is, as always, yours.

Let us take another example, this time that of Margaret Hilda Thatcher, the grocer's daughter who became Britain's first woman Prime Minister. Her date of birth is 13th October 1925.

Birth day	+	Birth month	+	Year of birth	=	Personal Number

Birth day	=	4 $(1 + 3 = 4)$
Birth month	=	10
Year of birth	=	8 $(1 + 9 + 2 + 5 = 17: 1 + 7 = 8)$
Personal Number	=	**4** $(4 + 10 + 8 = 22: 2 + 2 = 4)$

The power of four symbolizes the highest potential of individual endeavour and will. Intense application, total commitment, dogged determination and work, work, work, are all common characteristics and behaviours that are inspired by the number four potential. Margaret Thatcher displayed these qualities during her eleven years in office, to both the delight and despair of the nation.

Let us take one more example of a personal birthdate number, this time the Indian religious and political leader Mahatma Gandhi, who was born on 2nd October 1869.

Birth day	+	Birth month	+	Year of birth	=	Personal Number

Birth day	=	2
Birth month	=	10
Year of birth	=	6 $(1 + 8 + 6 + 9 = 24: 2 + 4 = 6)$
Personal Number	=	**9** $(2 + 10 + 6 = 18: 1 + 8 = 9)$

Mahatma Gandhi's personal birthdate number is the number nine. The potential behind the number nine inspires law and spiritual law, truth and spiritual truth, observation, discrimination and judgement. It also feeds dignity, honour, and the awareness of how important it is to set a good example in life. Mahatma Gandhi embraced all of these attributes and qualities. He studied law in England, pursued spiritual and political truth in Africa and

India, and led by example in whatever he endeavoured to change. In fact, it was Mahatma Gandhi who once said 'My teaching is my example.'

'Shadow Number'

In numerology there is a *Kingdom of Light* and also a *Kingdom of Shadows*. To put it another way, every number in your numerology profile has a *shadow number*, or *shadow power*, which is another potential you can call upon for strength and guidance. A central aim and challenge of numerology is to create an appropriate balance and harmony between your numbers and their shadow opposites.

The word 'shadow' is commonly used in certain schools of psychology, and also in drama and art, to convey either profundity or something sinister. In numerology the word 'shadow' does not in any way convey 'evil', 'badness', 'negativity', 'danger' or any other sinister overtone. As stated in Chapter One, there are no 'bad energies', 'unlucky fortunes', 'harmful vibes' or 'negative potentials' in numerology. The potentials of numbers become either 'good' or 'bad' depending on how well you accommodate and control them.

Therefore, in numerology the word 'shadow' refers to 'that which is hidden from normal view'. It points to inner, innate qualities which at first glance are not apparent or obvious to any meaningful degree. For example, if we liken our personal birthdate number to the tip of an iceberg, then beneath sea level there also exists, out of view, the 'shadow'—a vast, powerful body of potential and possibilities.

All of us have a 'shadow potential;' few of us realize it. Your personal birthdate number represents the *potential before you*, and also your *possible destiny*; your personal birthdate shadow number represents the *potential deep within you*, and also your *heritage*. To put it another way, your personal birthdate number represents that which you have come to work with and develop in life. It represents what you might become. Your personal birthdate shadow number represents on one level what you already have and what you already are.

The 'shadow' only turns to 'light' if you allow yourself to 'open up' to this potential. It represents specifically profound, innate, inner, deep qualities. These qualities are unlocked through careful contemplation and persistent nurturing. You do not *make* the 'shadow potential' work *for* you; rather, you *allow* it to work *through* you. You must be prepared, therefore, to 'open up' to it and to allow it to pour through you.

The shadow of number one is the number eight. The shadow of number two is the number seven. The shadow of number three is the number six. The shadow of number four is the number five. The shadow of five is the number four. The shadow of six is the number three. The shadow of seven is the number two. The shadow of eight is the number one. And the shadow of nine is nine. In fact, you can see that the personal birthdate number and its shadow always add up to the power of nine, which in numerology is the symbol for balance, alchemy, transmutation, completion and Law.

If we take a closer look, it is possible to see an exact relationship between the nine primary integers and their shadows. Briefly stated, the power of one may be said to represent material ambition. Its shadow power of eight inspires spiritual ambition. Briefly stated, the power of the two is a symbol for feeling and emotion. Its shadow power of seven is a symbol for Spiritual Love.

The power of three stands for reason and intelligence. Its shadow power of six represents wisdom and knowing.

The power of four promotes individual will and human endeavour. The power of five, its shadow potential, promotes collective will and spiritual endeavour. Therefore, the powers of one, two, three and four have a higher, spiritual reflection in eight, seven, six and five, respectively. Therefore, if your personal birthdate number is either one, two, three or four, then you should also be aware of its respective higher shadow potential.

If, however, your personal number is either five, six, seven or eight, the relationship to the shadow is slightly different. For instance, the potential of five, *collective will*, rarely amounts to much if it has not first been built upon the rock of four, *the potential of personal will*. How can we expect to serve a community if we cannot even serve ourselves? Also, the potential of six, that of *wisdom and knowing*, has to be earthed and supported by the potential of three. How can we trust our wisdom if we cannot trust our intelligence?

The potential of seven, that of *unconditional Love*, is nothing if we have not also learnt to feel, experience and live with emotion. The power of seven is like the butterfly that emerges from the chrysalis power of two. They are opposites, yet they are complementary and dependent upon one another for each other's existence. Likewise, the potential of eight, *spiritual success*, is rarely fully realized unless you have first fulfilled the power of one, *physical success*.

We can aim to avoid all of the numbers in our numerology chart, except for one, the power of nine. Those of us whose personal birthdate number is the nine potential, or who have a high occurrence of nines in our numerology chart, particularly three nines, cannot escape or ignore the nine potential, for it is before us, behind us and within us. Failure to acknowledge this power can, therefore, even be harmful. For this reason, nine is referred to as the *number of challenges.* On one level, though, it should be stated that each and every number is a number of challenges.

The significance of your shadow number will be as great as you allow it to be. However, it should be noted that the shadow potential of your personal birthdate number tends to be naturally more active and more evident in the later years of your life. In particular it is thought to blossom in the second and third stages of life. It is during these times of life that we are often prepared and interested enough to look beyond, to dig deeper and travel within ourselves a little more than before. We know where we are heading and what we have got, but where did we come from and with what? This is the time when the shadow potential often manifests naturally and almost of its own accord.

First, Second and Third Stages of Life

The existence of cycles or stages of life is an idea which is common to most cultures. Yogis and Hindus, for example, often talk of the four stages of life, and also describe life as a series of seven-year cycles. They are by no means the only cultures or civilizations that have supported the idea of cycles. The Greeks, Romans, Egyptians, North American Indians and Chinese also interpreted the pattern and progress of life through stages and cycles. Linear time and step-by-step history is a peculiar oddity of modern Western civilization which will soon be rectified. Evolution is, of course, cyclic by nature!

Let us, once again, take the example of Walt Disney, the American pioneer of cartoon films, whose birthdate is the 5th December 1901.

Birth day	+	Birth month	+	Year of birth	=	Personal Number

Birth day	=	5
Birth month	=	3 (12: 1 + 2 = 3)
Year of birth	=	2 (1 + 9 + 0 + 1 = 11: 1 + 1 = 2)
Personal Number	=	**1** (5 + 3 + 2 = 10: 1 + 0 = 1)

The personal birthdate number comprises a set of three numbers, each of which is a symbol for one of the three major stages of life, each stage lasting for about twenty-seven years (three nines). Nine nines stands for Law, for Completion, and also for Life.

The *birth day number(s)* represents the first stage of life. In other words, it symbolizes a potential for the first twenty-seven years of your life. The numbers one, two and three in your numerology chart can also be naturally more active throughout this time of *initiation*. During this first stage of life we do our best to establish a framework for living on Earth. To do so, we earth ourselves by establishing direction, setting a course, beginning a career, and by developing a physical, emotional and mental code of practice. Throughout all of this time, the birth day number will be a significant and perhaps highly evident potential and influence. Just as important will be its shadow potential.

Walt Disney may well have been influenced and supported by the potential of five and also by its shadow power of four during his first stage of life. Collective will is in the ascendant and therefore takes priority over personal will. The power of four can be an invaluable tower of strength and a foundation for the five potential. The four potential can turn a collective ideal into a powerful collective will, and ultimately into a possible collective reality.

The number(s) of the *birth month* represent potentials

and influences which may awaken and/or flourish in particular during the second stage of your life. The duration of this second stage is approximately another twenty-seven years. The numbers four, five and six in your numerology chart may also be naturally more active during this stage.

This second stage of life traditionally encompasses the *transition* from physical, emotional, mental individual priorities to philosophical, contemplative, spiritual collective priorities. The 'physical flush' has ended, or at least should have ended. The forty-fifth year, or thereabouts, is often a time of struggle between the individual and collective wills, and can often, therefore, herald the period commonly termed 'mid-life crisis'.

Walt Disney would have been influenced by the magical twelve, which, when calculated becomes $1 + 2 = 3$, or 'one, two, three'. The shadow potential of three is six, and the sum of one, two and three is also six. Also, the power of twelve can be arrived at by doubling the power of six. Therefore, twelve often stands for the successful transmutation of physical, emotional and mental reason into qualities of wisdom and knowing.

The number(s) of the *year of birth* represent possible potentials for the third stage of life. This number is active during the next twenty-seven years of your life, and thereafter until death. It represents, in particular, the *resolution* of your life and work. The numbers seven, eight and nine in your numerology chart may also be naturally more active during this time of life. Also, the shadow potentials will probably be more active and easier to access.

If we take the whole of Walt Disney's year of birth, we arrive at an interesting pattern of $(1 + 9) = 10 + 01 = 11 = 1 + 1 = 2$. A numerologist would be fascinated by the pattern of 1001 (10 + 01), which, roughly interpreted, describes a life which began with ambition and original flair (the potential of one), which made space for original-ity to manifest (the potential of two zeros), and which ended on the creative and original note with which it began (the potential of one again).

Walt Disney's personal birthdate number is the number one. However, if we begin to analyse all of the numbers that create his date of birth, as if to compile a numerology chart, then we can also see that the number one proliferates throughout, and therefore adds even more possible impact, meaning, significance and potential power to his life.

Your personal birthdate number is a very significant number, not least because it also contains the three num-bers that represent and symbolize the potentials and influ-ences that can motivate and characterize the three stages of life. Your personal birthdate number is by no means the whole truth, though. It holds a similar position to that of your Sun sign in astrology, in that while it is one of the most important of all influences it is by no means the only influence. Indeed, as with astrology, other potentials, life events and conditions can conspire so as to create a pattern which overrides your personal birthdate number.

It can also be the case that you connect more to the shadow potential of your personal birthdate number. The whole truth can only be arrived at via a complete numer-ology profile, and, of course, via the two most important ingredients of all, which are *experience* and *decision*. There can be no dogma or certainty in numerology, only poten-tial, possibilities and, at best, probabilities.

'Day/Night Baby', 'Sun/Moon Child'

The study of numerology suggests that we are each of us borne upon the tides of particular energies and potentials.

One such energy and potential has to do with the hour of our birth and whether or not we were born during the daytime or night-time. As with its sister science, astrology, numerology places great significance on the time of birth and on the phases of the Moon and Sun at birth.

The hour of birth has always been vested with significance, though by no means as great a significance as the personal birthdate number. It is said that each hour points to a direction and to a destiny in life. It is suggested that you should pay particular attention to the number of your hour of birth if a) this number is the same as your personal number, b) this number is the same as your shadow number, c) this number provides potentials that you do not have in your *personal name number*, or d) this number is the most repeated potential in your full numerology chart.

If you were born at night-time, you are a *night baby* or *Moon Child*. This means that, if you so choose, you can be empowered, influenced and inspired especially by the archetypes of night and of the Moon. The night and the Moon are symbols for feminine, intuitive, imaginative and right-brain power and potential. The silvery light of the night-time sky is a collective, nurturing, feeding energy. Very often it is linked with feminine creativity, with unconscious expression, and also with psychic control. It cools the fire of the Sun, and thereby creates and maintains physical as well as spiritual harmony.

If you were born during the daytime, you are a *day baby* or *Sun Child*. This means that, if you so choose, you can be empowered, influenced and inspired especially by the archetypes of day and of the Sun. The day and the Sun are symbols for masculine, initiating, reasoning and left-brain power and potential. The golden light of the daytime sky feeds and strengthens ambition, achievement, progress and endeavour. Very often it is linked with masculine creativity, with conscious expression and with physical control.

Of course, feminine potentials are by no means the exclusive right of a Moon Child, just as masculine potentials are by no means the exclusive right of a Sun Child. We are pointing only to potentials, possibilities and probabilities. There is no certainty in numbers, simply because it is up to us to make of our numbers what we will. All the potential in the world will not manifest while we do not act. There is an old saying that 'if a person takes one step towards God, God will take two steps towards you.' In numerology the same is true: *take one step towards your potential and your potential will take two steps towards you*.

Some people are born on the *cusp* of day and night, or the cusp of night and day. Here the two worlds of night and day and Sun and Moon are close together, and therefore dexterity, versatility and agile movement between them may be easy, and the marriage of the two potentials may be easier to achieve. Once again, though, it is we who must look for, discover and realize our potential.

We all of us operate better at some times than at others. Some of us work better at night-time, burning the midnight oil, unlike the majority who prefer to be active by day and passive by night. Some of us operate well in the mornings when we are full of vigour, drive and optimism. The afternoons may not be so good. Or perhaps we prefer afternoons to mornings?

Numerology suggests that each day is a miniature life, and that within each day there are times when we feel born, alive and awake to the world. There will also be times which are better than others for creative expression, decisions, inspiration or hard work, for example. Very often these times may correspond to your actual time of birth.

Masculine and Feminine Numbers

As explained in Chapter One, many of the ancient schools of numerology believed that the world is composed of, supported by and evolves through a dance of two essential forces of *masculine* and *feminine*. The power and potential of numbers is also, therefore, governed by the dance of masculine and feminine. This means essentially that some numbers have a stronger masculine potential, whereas others have a stronger feminine potential.

The primary masculine numbers are one, three, five and seven. The powers of one and three are material, physical potencies; whereas the powers of five and seven are higher, collective potencies. They are all, however, masculine potentials, and as such are linked to the day, the Sun, heat, fire, extroversion, yin, animus, activity, initiative, impregnation, ambition and endeavour. Masculine powers also strengthen and activate left-brain talents.

The primary feminine numbers are two, four, six and eight. The powers of two and four are material, physical potencies; whereas the powers of six and eight are higher, collective potencies. They are all, however, feminine potentials, and as such are linked to the night, the Moon, coolness, water, introversion, yang, anima, passivity, support, reception, nurturing and contemplation. Feminine powers also support and nurture right-brain talents.

Masculine and feminine numbers are, once again, tools which you will use either correctly or incorrectly, appropriately or inappropriately, constructively or destructively. Also, just as each separate number provides innate lessons and experiences, so too do the masculine and feminine powers behind each number.

The lesson of masculine and feminine is one of *complementarity* and of *appropriate balance*. Therefore, a man with a majority of masculine numbers in his chart must obviously harness the power of masculine, but not at the expense of the feminine. This is because masculine and feminine cannot and do not survive, live or prosper without one another. Appropriate acknowledgment of his femininity will, therefore, support his masculinity. The relationship of masculine and feminine is a relationship of *complementary opposites*.

The same lessons of complementarity and appropriate balance apply to a woman with a majority of feminine numbers in her chart. She must harness her feminine potential, but not exclusively so. Too much femininity ruins a character, just as too much masculinity ruins a character. Just as the Earth relies upon a balance of Sun and Moon, so too do we rely on a balance of masculine and feminine. Appropriate acknowledgment of her masculinity will, therefore, strengthen her femininity.

The study of numerology and the study of life are but one and the same discipline. Both studies teach that the potentials of masculine and feminine belong to each and every one of us. Some potentials come to us more easily than others. Very often, though, the potentials that we have to work most hard to realize are often the most valuable. Whatever your gender, you have both masculine and feminine potentials. A study of numbers and a day-to-day relationship with numbers can help you realize these potentials, because numerology teaches you that *you are all possibilities*.

CHAPTER FOUR

YOUR PERSONAL NAME NUMBER

In the Beginning...

In the beginning was the Word, and the Word was with God, and the Word was God.

John: 1

Throughout our world there are wonderful, rich and descriptive legends, myths, stories and tales which describe the Creation of the World as an event encompassing sound, music, vibrations and *The Word*: 'In the beginning was the Word, and the Word was with God, and the Word was God'. This description is by no means exclusive to the Christian tradition.

In ancient Hindu scriptures reference is made to the *Song of Creation*. Frequent allusion is also made to *The Word*, which in the ancient language of Sanskrit was *OM*, or *A-U-M*. It is interesting to note that Sanskrit was more of a sound system than a written language. Names, speech, songs, hymns and mantras were all considered holy to the ancient Hindu because 'all is vibration, and all vibration is holy,' because it was believed to emanate from God, or *Brahma*. Sound and vibration are, therefore, everything. This belief is neatly expressed in the *Vakya Padiya*: 'In this

Universe, there is no form of knowledge which is not perceived through sound; knowledge is pierced through by sound; all this Universe is but the result of sound.'

The Word belongs also to African mythology. In *The Origin of Life and Death*, edited by Ulli Beier, there is a passage which begins,

> The sky was large, white, and very clear. It was empty; there were no stars and no moon; only a tree stood in the air and there was wind. This tree fed on the atmosphere and ants lived on it. Wind, tree ants, and atmosphere were controlled by the power of the Word. But the Word was not something that could be seen. It was a force that enabled one thing to create another.

In the oriental holy script, the *Tao te Ching*, there is also reference to sound, vibration and to 'the named' as playing an active part 'in the beginning...' To be a Sage, or wise person, the *Tao te Ching* advises that you respect the power behind words and names, and that you should use words only very rarely: 'To use words but rarely, is to be natural,' we are told. And as for 'in the beginning...'

> The nameless was the beginning of heaven and earth;
> The named was the mother of the myriad creatures.

Tao te Ching, page 57

Examples abound in the mythologies, philosophies and religions of the world that tell of the importance and reverence attached to the power of The Word, of vibration, sound and also of 'the named'. Similar examples have been unearthed from the North American, Greek and Egyptian traditions, for example, where the powers of creation, magic, healing and good fortune were considered to be locked up in the vibrational power that can be supported, transported and activated by words and by names.

What's in a Name?

> *Juliet: Bondage is hoarse, and may not speak aloud.*
> *Else would I tear the cave where Echo lies.*
> *And make her airy tongue more hoarse than mine.*
> *With repetition of my Romeo's name.*
> *Romeo: It is my soul that calls upon my name.*

William Shakespeare, *Romeo and Juliet*, II. ii.

All is arranged according to number. Everything is subject to not only the laws of vibration but also to the laws of numbers. Nothing is left out; not even a name. That the whole world can be described, interpreted and understood through the inner philosophy and hidden meaning of numbers is the most fundamental law of numerology. *All is arranged according to number*.

In numerology every name has a number, and every number has a name. A name carries an inner significance, a hidden meaning and a personal wisdom. Today, a name is our label; in the past, a name was our identity. Today we choose a name because it sounds good, it suits us and we respect it; in the past, a name was chosen for, among other things, its vibrational properties—and where numerology was practised, for its numerological potential.

In numerology the vibration of a name is of chief importance. In some traditions it was believed that a name was a personal key to enlightenment, freedom and ascension. Your name was likened to a *mantra* or a prayer.

Repeat it often enough and you would activate its power. It is interesting to note a case from more modern times: the nineteenth-century poet, Alfred Lord Tennyson found that if he repeated his name often enough he was soon moved to receive inspiration for his writing.

In some cultures, invoking a person's name was considered equal to invoking the power of that person. If, therefore, one meditated or contemplated upon the name of a person, or even upon the name of an animal, tree or stone, one could attune to and assume the properties of that person, animal or thing. This was deemed possible because *all* [numbers included] *is vibration, and all vibration is One*.

To meditate and to contemplate upon the vibration and the meaning of your own name was also considered a religious practice in some places of our ancient past. This practice was deemed to quicken the path of self-knowledge, self-control and self-realization. To know the number of your name was a distinct advantage and rare privilege. For this reason it was often made available only to those who had passed through a rite of initiation.

In the knighthood and heraldry of the West your name was your crest. To defend the honour of your name was considered vital, especially because it was the custom to pass on your name to your offspring. Your name was not yours; you were its custodian. The power and potential of your name would serve you only as well as you would serve it.

In many Eastern traditions people accept a name as part of an initiation into a religious order, church or sect. The Sufis, Tibetans, Buddhists and Yogis often choose to adopt this practice. The North American Indians had a similar system of names. By giving a person a new, spiritual name, that person has a new energy, vibration and power. This name is often aligned to a god, goddess or archetype which will help, protect and inspire a person along his or her path. A spiritual name is also a constant reminder of a person's original, spiritual identity: *invoke the name, and you also invoke that spiritual aspect of yourself.*

Chronological Order

Although significance is given to the power, vibration and meaning that lies behind a name, numerology tends to invest more importance in and greater consideration for dates. There are several fundamental reasons for this, one of which is that *names are subject to change; dates remain the same.*

By law you can change your name whenever you wish. Also, in your everyday life it is highly probable that you answer to any number of names. You own the full name on your birth certificate. You are sometimes called by your first name, but also, at other times, by your surname. You may have a nickname and more than one pet name. There are also maiden names and married names, and sometimes even a mix of the two.

Also, in certain countries, such as Poland, it is common to play word games with a name to express fondness, wishes, seniority, etc. Therefore the name Lilla can become Lilusia, Lileczka, Lilcia, Lilunia, Lilka, Liluncia, and so on! Unlike names, no matter how hard we might wish to change our date of birth the fact remains that the date stands and is unalterable. The German dramatist Bertolt Brecht once wrote, 'Don't take action because of a name! A name is an uncertain thing, you can't count on it!' (*A Man's a Man*, 1927). Names have an importance, then, but dates are always more significant.

To assess the numerological power and potential of

your names it is best to conduct a chronological investigation. First on the list, therefore, is your full name as given on your birth certificate. Next in order of importance is the name you answer to most often. If you are Richard, do you respond to Richard, Rich, Ricky, etc.? Or perhaps you answer to Mr or Dr Davies? In the former case you would include the letters 'm' and 'r' in your equations. Or maybe you have a nickname?

If you have changed your name through marriage, it is interesting to compare your maiden name with your newly married one, if you have chosen to discard your maiden name. If you have decided to take your maiden name into marriage, then measure this as well. There is a reason for everything you do. Most of these reasons can be based on instinct, intuition or feeling, and are, therefore, slightly removed from your normal conscious decision-making processes. Often, when it comes to a name, it simply feels right. By working out the number behind the name you may learn why it feels right for you.

As for the importance and significance that you should attach to your *personal name number* the advice given for your hour of birth also applies here. You should pay particular attention to the numbers of your name if a) this number is the same as your personal number, b) this number is the same as your shadow number, c) this number provides potentials that you do not have in your personal name number, or d) this number is the most repeated potential in your full numerology chart.

Another helpful numerology guideline for names is that the name you associate and are associated with, and which you and others use most often, is the active name energy in your life. This, therefore, is the name which you should use to identify your name vibration, or personal name number. The name used most often is most often the name you resonate to. This resonation may be decoded and translated through the language of numbers.

Personal Number Signatures

1. Ambition
2. Intuition
3. Reason
4. Will
5. Humanity
6. Wisdom
7. Love
8. Spirit
9. Discrimination

The Pythagorian Formula

The Greek philosopher and mathematician Pythagoras created the *Pythagorian Chart* to identify the numbers behind names. The Chart quite clearly aligns the letters of the alphabet to one of the primary nine integers. Therefore, the letters A, J and S each vibrate to the power of one; the letters B, K and T are each supported by the power of two; the power of three is linked to each of the letters, C, L and U, etc.

```
1 2 3 4 5 6 7 8 9
A B C D E F G H I
J K L M N O P Q R
S T U V W X Y Z
```

To achieve your own personal name number is a relatively straightforward mathematical task. You simply add all the numbers of your first name to get a single figure, and then add that number to a final single figure of your surname. Add these two figures together and you arrive at your personal name number.

In Chapter Two we explored the personal birthdate number of Walt Disney, the American pioneer of cartoons. Now we shall analyse the numbers behind the name.

W A L T
5 + 1 + 3 + 2
= 11 = 2

D I S N E Y
4 + 9 + 1 + 5 + 5 + 7
= 31 = 4

Name Number = 4 + 2 = **6**

Walt Disney's personal name number is the power of six, the symbol for wisdom and knowing. Walt Disney does not have a power of six anywhere in his personal birthdate number, except as a shadow power to the single number three. Therefore, the number six which supports his name will have perhaps been a useful tool of balance for him. That Walt Disney pursued wisdom there is no doubt.

If one digs a little deeper, a numerologist would be fascinated by the occurrence of five number ones in the numbers which are arranged in his name. This compares with twelve number ones that appear in the calculations for his personal birthdate number. Therefore, while six is a very significant influence in his personal name number, a numerologist would not discount or ignore the influence of the number one, which is, by its many appearances, undoubtedly a candidate for his *ruling influence*.

The example of Walt Disney is also of interest here

because his original name was Walter Elias, which when added up comes to a power of four. Walt Disney made, therefore, what was probably the unconscious choice of replacing the number four with the number six. It is also interesting to note that Walter Elias has six number ones. Perhaps Walt Disney felt he could afford to dispense with one number one!

Let us take another example, this time Albert Einstein, the German-American mathematician and physicist. His personal name number calculations appear below.

$$
\begin{array}{ccccccc}
A & L & B & E & R & T \\
1 + & 3 + & 2 + & 5 + & 9 + & 2 \\
& & = 22 = 4
\end{array}
$$

$$
\begin{array}{ccccccccc}
E & I & N & S & T & E & I & N \\
5 + & 9 + & 5 + & 1 + & 2 + & 5 + & 9 + & 5 \\
& & & = 41 = 5
\end{array}
$$

Name Number = 4 + 5 = **9**

Albert Einstein's personal name number is nine, a symbol for Law, discrimination, research and Supreme Intelligence. It would seem that Albert Einstein made full use of the nine potential in his life. The name (or vibration) of Einstein is today synonymous in many people's minds with intelligence. It is also certainly true that Albert Einstein was preoccupied with the study and research of laws.

There are at least two other interesting points about Albert Einstein's personal name number. The first point has to do with the presence of four nines. The relationship of the number four to the number nine can best be described as will (four) guided by the pursuit of Law, research and high endeavour (nine). It is highly likely, therefore, that with an arrangement of numbers such as these, every ounce of effort would be donated to the research of truth and of law.

The second point refers to the occurrence of six fives. The power of five is a symbol of the collective, of community and humanity, and the power of six is a symbol of wisdom and knowing. Six fives may therefore be interpreted as wisdom of humanity. Einstein was nothing if he was not a humanitarian. His work *Mein Weltbild*, or *The World As I See It*, is, for example, praised as a most profound philosophical and political picture of man.

Let us take one more example, this time Carl Jung, the Swiss psychologist. His personal name number appears below.

$$C \quad A \quad R \quad L$$
$$3 + 1 + 9 + 3$$
$$= 16 = 7$$
$$J \quad U \quad N \quad G$$
$$1 + 3 + 5 + 7$$
$$= 16 = 7$$

Name Number= 7 + 7 = 14 = 5

Carl Jung's personal name number is the number five. This seems remarkably appropriate for a man who is famous for his theories of *collective man* and the *collective unconscious*, for the number five symbolizes the power of the collective, of community and humanity. Carl Jung was a great traveller. He visited many of the primitive cultures of the world for first-hand experience and research. He considered himself a world citizen. Number five people often consider themselves as such, and are usually influenced by a desire to travel. It is interesting to note that even if we add Carl Jung's middle name, Gustav, to his personal name number calculations, the number is still five, because Gustav adds up to nine.

There are three threes in Carl Jung's personal name number. Thus the powers of reason and intellect (three) and also the powers of research, discrimination and the pursuit of Law (three threes add up to nine) are a part of the full potential of the name. It is quite clear that Carl Jung tapped this potential in his lifetime. There are also five ones. This suggests that the power of ambition (one) could have been motivated by the power of humanity (five). Carl Jung's ambition was not a personal ambition; it was an ambition for humanity.

Titles

The bestowing of titles by a community upon its peoples is a common, worldwide practice. Titles for humanitarianism, bravery, loyalty, nobility, inspired works, service, leadership or accomplishment are generally well known and well thought of. To aspire to receiving a title of some kind is not unknown to many of us.

It is a common observation that many people change their behaviour in the light of such awards. They are different people once they have been awarded a title of honour. This is partly because their self-image has changed, and also because their duties and responsibilities have changed. It has also to do with the fact that they have assumed a new name, and therefore a new name number and a new vibration.

Once again, in the past much more attention to detail was given to ritual than is so today. In ancient times great power and belief was vested in a ritual. It was believed, for example, that a ritual could change, heal, uplift, strengthen and transform a person. Ritual was all about the manipulation of power—the power that is always around us, never seen and hardly ever used. The bestowing of titles was one such ritual. The ritual was not so much about the title but rather about the power and the vibration behind that title. Numerologists interpreted this power and vibration through the system of numbers.

Place Names

House names, company names, team names, building names, street names, and the names of villages, towns, cities, regions, countries, continents, Planets, Solar Systems and Galaxies can all be read and understood according to numbers. All things, if they can be named, have a power, potential and number. This is the law of numerology.

The whole world is, of course, cluttered and filled with names. It is therefore possible to go quite overboard with name numbers, and also with house numbers, telephone numbers, insurance numbers, medical numbers, etc. The guiding rule is to attend to the names that resonate most with you and with which you come into contact most often in your life.

If you resonate to a particular name in your life; if you aspire to travel to a particular place in the world; if you have felt drawn to live in a certain city, town, street or house; if you have felt compelled to call your house a certain name—these are all very good reasons for looking up the number of a name. The order of importance may best be determined by the strength of your conscious resonations. For example, if the reason you moved to a house was because of the city and not the road, then the city name will most likely be more significant for you and to you.

It is also an interesting exercise to see how often your personal number or name number appears in your surroundings. This can be useful to assess how predominant a certain power is in your life. Once again, do not go overboard. Deciphering the name of your cat may be acceptable if, for instance, that name has resonated with you before your cat was alive. If, however, you have sixteen cats, a dog and a terrapin, you are best advised not to bother!

CHAPTER FIVE

THE CYCLES OF LIFE

Life, the passage of time, evolves through a glorious and grand design of cycles upon cycles upon cycles. Time, the units of life, is not the sequential, linear, A-to-B-to-C experience we measure with a watch or clock, but rather an organic, living pattern of experiences and lessons which evolve and revolve one around the other. This is a fundamental tenet of numerology.

The idea of life being a collection of experiences that evolves through cycles or stages is not exclusive to the science of numerology nor to its sister science, astrology. One of the best known examples of a way of life which embraces the philosophy of life cycles belongs to the Hindus and is described as the *Four Stages of Life*, or *Four Orders*. The first stage is the *way of the student*, during which you are, as a young person, initiated into the way of the world and also into the fundamental philosophical precepts of life. The second stage is the *way of the householder*, during which time you aim to practise and to integrate spiritual ethics, morals and values throughout your family life, both as spouse and as parent.

The third stage is the *way of the hermit*. During this time you aim to journey through your interior worlds, contemplating and meditating on the spiritual and the poetic, the philosophical and the eternal. The fourth and final stage is the *way of the ascetic*, which begins when your children have left the nest and your duties as a householder are effectively over. During this time you aim to renounce the physical world and embrace the spiritual one.

'Nine Lives'

There are essentially nine major life cycles in numerology, all of which you may live through, depending on your lifespan. These major cycles may be best described as *periods of specific potential and opportunity*. Each major cycle has a theme, and during the time of each cycle you are offered a set of specific experiences and lessons through which you journey in order to grow, develop and mature.

Each major life cycle is governed by a ruling number. The *Physical Cycle* is governed by the number one, the *Emotional Cycle* by the number two, the *Mental Cycle* by the number three, the *Endeavour Cycle* by the number four, the *Collective Cycle* by the number five, the *Wisdom Cycle* by the number six, the *Love Cycle* by the number seven, the *Spiritual Cycle* by the number eight, and the *Law Cycle* by the number nine.

A basic principle of numerology is that no number operates in isolation. Therefore, while the ruling number (and its shadow) is a very significant potential during the time of a major cycle, it is by no means the only number of influence for that time. First and foremost, there comes your personal birthdate number and its shadow. There is also the influence of your personal name number to consider. *Both these potentials live with you, no matter whatever, whenever or wherever*.

As well as these numbers there are the numbers of the *minor cycles*, which operate through all the individual major cycles. These minor cycles are the cycles of years, months and days. Each year of your life, as well as each month and each day, and even each minute, is governed by a potential that is symbolized by a number. You may like to refer to the later chapter of this book, which discuss these numbers in detail.

It is most important to comprehend that you do not, for instance, have to wait for the sixth major cycle in your life to experience and learn about wisdom. Nor do you have to bide your time until your third cycle before you begin to explore your mental potential. *All potentials are with you at all times.* The point is that when a number is particularly active in your life, as during a major life cycle, for instance, then the potential symbolized by that number is even more prominent and perhaps therefore even more significant and evident to you.

Your Physical Cycle

The time of your physical cycle supports, nurtures and promotes the growth and maturation of your physical body. Your physical body is a carriage for your mind and for you, the spirit. Physical agility, strength and skills are developed during this time, attributes that will be a support to your emotional, mental and spiritual growth. The health of your body is also of paramount importance during your physical cycle.

Your physical cycle lasts from the time of your birth up until and including eighteen years of age. During this time the potential symbolized by the number one may easily be activated, given the right conditions. Number one is traditionally associated with life, life-power, life-force, kundalini, climax, and also with birth and rebirth. It is also traditionally associated with the impregnation of spirit into matter.

The physical cycle and the power of the number one mark a time for arrival, beginnings and setting your stall out in life. During this time the potentials around you lead you into your physical existence. You immerse yourself thoroughly in the world, and translate what you experience mostly through your physical senses and feelings. In more ancient times, in particular, physical adeptness meant physical survival.

The time of your physical cycle is also a time of firsts. *First-hand* experience and *first attempts* are your teachers; *coming first* or *getting a first* may be your priority; *first come, first served* may be your philosophy; impulsive *first impressions* may be your guiding star; and you, perhaps more so than at any other time in your life, are *first and foremost* at the centre of the world. The time of your physical cycle may also herald other firsts, such as your first car, first job or first love.

Physical aptitude and success in sport may be a feature of your life during this time. If you are particularly keen and good at what you do, you may find that sport and recreation continue to feature for much or all of your life. You will find that as you live through the various life cycles to come your attitude and approach to what you do may change accordingly. For instance, during your third cycle you may adopt a more mental, thoughtful and strategic approach, and during your fourth and fifth cycles you may turn your hand to coaching, team building and management.

The physical cycle promotes the qualities of the child in us all. Unconditional love, innocence, appreciation, thankfulness, a fresh pair of eyes for everything, original- ity, creativity, trust, joy, an appetite for life, spirit, zest and hope are qualities many of us experience during childhood and at the time of the physical cycle. We each of us often make the mistake, however, of neglecting these qualities later in life when they could serve us so well.

There is often a determined influence and pressure to make a first attempt to plan your life's direction during your physical cycle. It can be a time when, especially towards the end of the cycle, you may begin to formulate and create plans, paths and projections for the future. The first sign of a future blueprint for your life may reveal itself to you during this time.

Making an impact on life, perceiving ourselves as successful, and hopefully having other people see us in a similar light are often key priorities during the time of the physical cycle. Material ambitions, wishes for wealth, physical attractions and flights of fame and fortune are the stuff life is made of for many of us throughout this time.

Paradoxically, the time of the physical cycle can be when you first begin to catch a glimpse and a glimmer of a spiritual understanding and experience of the world around you. This can be particularly so if you are significantly influenced in your chart by the number eight, shadow to the number one. The time of eighteen is when the number one (physical) and the number eight (spiritual) meet and are ruled by a nine ($1 + 8 = 9$: Law).

The spiritual surfaces in your life for perhaps the first time around the age of eighteen and a bit before, and traditionally, therefore, this is potentially a time when physical, emotional, mental and spiritual confusion, indecision or sudden change of direction may arise. Once again, much of this also depends upon prevailing conditions in your life, the dominant numbers in your chart, and also upon your past experiences and lessons.

The physical cycle, therefore, represents your entrance into the world. It is a time when the power and potential of the number one is particularly active, helping to formulate your identity, foster and encourage your understanding, mature your immediate potential and establish a firm footing for the future. *A building is only as strong as its foundations*, and therefore the influence of your first major cycle has a particularly profound affect on you. *It was the child you were that helped make you the adult you are.*

Your Emotional Cycle

Your emotional cycle is the second major life cycle you experience. It encompasses the nine years of life between the ages of 19 and 27. Unlike the physical cycle, which is ruled by a masculine potential, your emotional cycle is ruled by a feminine potential, as symbolized by the number two. The potential of two may easily be realized during the emotional cycle, for better or for worse.

During the second, emotional cycle of your life you aim to build upon the first, physical cycle. Successes and strengths, weaknesses and failures, all are carried over from one cycle to the next throughout your life. Throughout each of the cycles you will be collecting credits and/or debits, accruing dividends and/or debts, and receiving interest and/or arrears. Numerological lore states quite clearly that *no number and no cycle can be strong on its own*.

Just as your physical cycle is often a time of firsts, your emotional cycle is often a cycle of seconds. You may find you are spurred on towards your success by a *second wind* during this cycle. Alternatively, this may be a time for self-doubt, inner confusion, disorientation and *second thoughts*. Many of us learn our most painful lessons during the emotional cycle. A *second childhood* is also not out of the question.

It is often during the time of two, in your emotional cycle, that you, as an individual, will join with another to make two. During the physical cycle the emphasis has usually been orientated around your individual self. You are, to coin the phrase, young, free and single. In the emotional cycle the emphasis often alters through your life experiences so as to focus on joining, connection and relationship.

Whereas your relationships may be motivated by physical attraction in the physical cycle, your relationships are likely to be motivated more by emotional empathy in the emotional cycle. Emotional growth is often painful and traumatic. To live through the emotional cycle can be to live through adversity. Therefore, the desire for emotional stability, comfort and soothing may be particularly pleasing during this time. While it can be appropriate at times to let your emotions guide you, it is most important to ensure that they do not rule you.

The potential as symbolized by the power of two is a potential of duality. Therefore, the second cycle in your life can easily be a time of tension and turmoil. This is particularly so if you have not come to terms with your own relationship to yourself. During this cycle all of us may have to attempt to come to terms with the question *How can I expect to live with and love another person if I cannot yet learn to live with and love myself?*

On the other hand, when a relationship is open, trusting and creative many people find they become more independent during the time of two than in the time of one. By caring for and loving others, individuals often find that they can care for and love themselves that much better. This may be true for people who are particularly influenced by the power of seven in their chart, which symbolizes a potential for unconditional love. At the age of twenty-seven, the number two and the number seven meet one another. They are ruled by the nine, and therefore this year in your life is often a time for very serious decision and discrimination.

Acknowledging your feminine nature can be either a testing time or a revelation and source of great happiness during the second major cycle of your life. Creativity, sensitivity, intuition, inspiration and soul may all be alive during this time, particularly if you work at allowing these potentials to flow through you. Emotional experience, be it painful or happy, is often the inspiration for art, philosophy, poetry and wisdom.

The feminine in us has a store for our soul and psychic dimensions. We describe those who are psychic as having the gift of *second sight*. Very often, during your second major cycle of life you may begin to attune yourself to the psychic and spiritual dimensions of your self. The spiritual may easily be very active and very meaningful to you if you are influenced significantly by the numbers five, six, seven, eight and/or nine in your numerology chart.

The time of two is also a time for decisions. The decisions you make during the time of two are often the decisions that stick with you for life. The second cycle of your life is an extremely fertile time. Our characters, personality, attributes and failures are all sculpted by the experience of emotion. Controlling and protecting your emotions, as best you are able, will help you to realize more of the potential of your future cycles. Like the physical cycle, the emotional cycle is another cycle of foundation for this world.

Your Mental Cycle

For the nine years that span the ages of twenty-eight and thirty-six you experience the third major cycle of your life, which is the mental cycle. During your first cycle physical aptitude and success often take a lead in your life, and may be, depending on other influences in your chart, the only things you desire and reach out for. During your second cycle the tendency is for emotional strength and stability to be the order of the day; these assets are therefore prized and valued, to an extent determined by the other numerological influences in your life.

During your third cycle, however, the emphasis may change again, this time to centre around your mental world and the development and maturation of your mental skills. Once again, if the number three or six is prevalent in your personal birthdate number or personal name number, for instance, then the emphasis on mental success and mental values will be all the more great—maybe even a little too great!

Very often it is during your third life cycle that mental performance and aptitude flourish, perhaps particularly in the workplace. The potential of three, which is dominant during your third cycle, is a masculine, initiating and outgoing energy. It is a potential that is often linked to success, to *third time lucky*, and also to good fortune through hard work.

It can be quite easy during this time for notions of mental success to be superseded by notions of mental superiority. Ambition, pride, avarice, boastfulness and conceit are all common failings which are often associated either with having too many threes in your life or with imbalance and upset during the time of three. When we fail to take control of the three potential, we may sometimes be accused of being a little too hard-nosed for our own good, and also of allowing self-interest to take a front seat too often. Beware!

During your first cycle physical attraction is often the prime motivation and enjoyment in relationships; during your second cycle emotional empathy and bonding often play Cupid's arrow; but during your mental cycle it is often a meeting of minds that forms the main attraction.

While mental attraction is by no means exclusive to the time of your third life cycle, there is a strong tendency and a definite potential for mental appreciation and mental cohesion to lead the way during this time, or indeed during any other time of three.

Relationships can become more and more fulfilling as you move through life cycles together. When there is physical, emotional and mental attraction in a relationship this is often a sign of a deep and strong friendship. A marriage of minds (in one form or another) is often vital to long-term success in relationships. However, it can be a failing to allow the mental to dominate too much.

If we are honest with ourselves, we know we are all susceptible at times in our lives to staying on the mental perch either too much or for too long. Emotions are often risky; the mind appears a safe haven. Yet we know deep within ourselves that a relationship controlled by the mental and devoid of emotion is rarely a formula for fulfilment. To live in the mind may appear to be safe, but sometimes it may be apt to ask ourselves *is living in the mind really living?*

There can also be a tendency during the third cycle of your life to allow the rational, logical and analytical to dominate and overrule the intuitive, instinctive and imaginative. Once again, there is apparent safety in the rational, apparent risk in the intuitive. *Rewards are refused when risk is not proffered.*

The age of thirty-six is the time when the number three (mental) meets its shadow number six (wisdom) and both are ruled by the number nine ($3 + 6 = 9$: Law). This, then, is often a fertile time for mental and personal growth, development and transformation.

Your third life cycle is vital for the evolution of the mind. Like every other cycle in your life, it brings with it certain experiences and lessons. It is potentially a time of great growth and personal success. The mind leads the way as it matures, strengthens and develops. However, *the mind of you is not the whole of you*. Do not, therefore, let your mind eclipse the part of you that is feeling, emotional, soulful, feminine and creative. True mental strength will allow you to encompass and integrate all of these dimensions of yourself.

Your Endeavour Cycle

Your fourth major life cycle is the cycle of endeavour, which lasts for the nine years from thirty-seven up to and including forty-five. You have now travelled through the first three major cycles of your life, gathering experiences, learning lessons and establishing strengths—physical, emotional and mental ones. Now, in your fourth major life cycle, you have a chance to draw these strengths together, to consolidate them and, through the powers of endeavour and application, dedicate yourself wholeheartedly to life.

The nine years of your fourth major life cycle can be very productive years for you, in all departments of your life. Your body of will is feeding you with the strength and determination to apply yourself in a more mature and consistent way than ever before. During these years you will learn that one of the greatest keys to success and happiness is work.

You may also find that as well as greater strength and determination you also gain a greater vision and direction. You have had time to think about what it is you really want to do with your life, and now you may find that your enthusiasm, dedication and devotion to a cause or causes is your greatest strength. You are prepared to work hard, and what is more, you know what it is you want to work hard for.

The ability to work well is a wonderful, liberating strength; the mistake to work only and always can let you down badly. Do not allow yourself to become a slave to the wheel of labour. The need to be successful is sometimes more important to us than the need to live, quite literally. By being addicted to work we are often getting ready to live, but never really, in the fullest sense of the word, living. Spare a thought for the quality in your life. What does quality mean to you? Do you get enough of it? *Today, I shall spare a thought for quality*.

You may find that your approach to life alters during your fourth life cycle. If you have felt you have been a victim of life up until now, you may begin to feel you are ready to assume the role of adept and controller. Now is the time to assess your strengths and your weaknesses, and to use them all to help propel yourself forward in life. Your weaknesses are only hindrances to you if they are not carefully protected, nurtured and understood. Take time to know what they are and how exactly they affect you—you will then find that you can begin to control them more than they control you.

The power of four rules your fourth cycle. It is traditionally linked to the geometric designs of cross and square—both of which have been described throughout the cultures of the world as symbols of support, foundation and building. During your fourth life cycle you may find you support yourself better than at any time previously. You may also find, therefore, that you are in a better position to support others. While you are making the most of your life you can be helping others to make the most of theirs.

It is during your fourth major life cycle that you can earth yourself well. If, perhaps, your approach to life thus far has been motivated by the spiritual, the aesthetic, the creative, the artistic and the religious, you may be in danger of floating off the surface of the earth! You may now find that by earthing yourself more, by *getting down on all fours*, you will create a foundation which supports you all the more. Keep your head up high towards the stars, by all means, but keep your feet planted firmly on the ground.

Relationships can be very productive for you during your fourth major life cycle. You may find you approach relationships with a greater strength and realism than before. You may find, for instance, that working for romance brings with it many rewards. The harder you work to create, strengthen or preserve a bond, the stronger that bond often becomes. You will be learning all the time that *when you work for life, life works for you*.

Achievement is a keynote for the time of your cycle of endeavour. The field of your achievement is largely up to you—occupations, careers, relationships, personal or spiritual development, travel, education, family, etc. Careful consideration supports dogged determination. Plan, project, organize and forecast exactly what it is you are prepared to work for, and then work at it until you achieve it. The locus of control is not *out there*, it's *in you*. If you work for this reality it must become your reality.

The most crucial time of your life cycle happens at forty-five—the age that is traditionally assigned to mid-life crisis. At forty-five, or thereabouts, your life stops, momentarily, at a full fulcrum point. The number four, the potential of personal will, meets face to face with its shadow number five, potential of collective will. The number four, the potential of individual causes, meets the number five, potential of group causes. The number four, the potential of earthing, endeavour and physical effort, meets the number five, the potential of spiritual, soulful and philosophical pursuit. The number four and the number five add up to and are ruled by nine. In other words, you must discriminate, weigh up and decide. You are the child; the world is your family; life is your parent. What will you do now? A re-birth and greater maturity and realization, or a second childhood?

During the fourth major life cycle you may discover a greater understanding of what it is to be personally very strong and successful. A part of that understanding, according to the philosophy of four and five, is that the truly strong person forsakes the petty, individual ambition and will for the greater, collective and more meaningful ambition and will of the world. Collective responsibilities transcend personal gains. It is now, during the fourth major life cycle, that you encounter a potential which can establish you as a new kind of citizen—*a citizen of the world*.

Your Collective Cycle

The fifth major cycle of your life begins on the first day of forty-six and ends on the last day of fifty-four, lasting, once again, for a period of nine years. Much of what happens during this cycle depends upon what has passed before. A bumpy entrance into your collective cycle may mean a bumpy ride for some time. A smooth exit from your endeavour cycle might set you up for truly astonishing experiences that will surpass your own hopes and expectations.

The fifth major life cycle is renowned for being a time of re-birth and new growth. It is often during this cycle that you might either discover your first true vocation in life or set sail for an entirely new destination and port of call. We each of us have a tremendous capacity to surprise ourselves. At no time is this more true than during the moments that mark the passage of your major and minor collective cycles.

The collective cycle is governed by the number five, which is a symbol for a potential with astonishing versatility. During your collective cycle you may discover talents that are entirely new to you, or you may find that you surpass yourself at old talents. Who you were and who you become during this cycle may be two completely different people. Adventure often rides high during the time of five, and you may discover within yourself a whole new adventure which previously either was not there or was not perceived.

Your collective cycle promotes such versatile potential because of the support and strength of foundation you established during your first four major life cycles. Physical experience, emotional experience and mental experience, as acquired in the first three major life cycles, has been the inspiration behind the personal endeavour you experience during your fourth major life cycle. Now the final act, that of aligning yourself to greater causes than that of your own, is part of the potential of this new major life cycle.

The relationship between four and five represents one of the most dramatic relationships in all of numerology. As mentioned previously, the numbers one to four represent the journey from spirit into matter; the numbers five to nine represent the return journey from matter to spirit. Whereas the first four numbers mark the birth and development of the individual and of individual causes; the next five numbers mark the appearance of the collective world and of collective causes. Personal responsibility now means collective responsibility. A part of the challenge of this time is to contemplate these things and then to rise to action.

Whereas *direction* was absolutely vital to you during

your first four major life cycles, you may now find that it is *purpose* that you need. In other words, any old direction might have done in the past, but now any old direction will not do at all. Purpose is the keynote for this time. That which you aim to do and that which you achieve must have a meaning, a significance and a purpose to you. From now on purpose underlines your character and motivates your actions.

During the time of five you will often find that, although it may not be your motive, your own personal needs are met more fully when you forsake them for the needs of another or of a greater cause. You have established yourself now, so now is the time to work for others and help them establish themselves. How you do this is up to you. It may happen through a position in management, an attempt at politics, voluntary work, support for a charity, training work, environmental causes, spiritual vocations, or within the family, for instance.

Another experience which may occur during your collective cycle is that your perceived weaknesses and sensitivities, which for so long have weighed you down, may now transform themselves so as to serve as your greatest strengths and attributes. Like the butterfly that emerges from the chrysalis, it sometimes happens that the very things which you have felt have tied you down now liberate you. Perceptions alter: experiences alter. Now is a time to challenge perceptions of yourself and of the world around you.

Inwardly you may experience many subtle changes during the time of five. The greatest challenge of all is to allow yourself to feel and experience things differently. Imagine you are starting all over again. Make no assumptions, cast off your old robes of conditioning. Perceive yourself no longer as an individual island, but as someone who is connected intimately with, who is a part of all the lands, seas and skies. Your strength as an individual will, during these specific times, be derived from the strength you impart to the people and to the causes in the world around you.

Your Wisdom Cycle

The nine years that make up your sixth major life cycle are the wisdom years. During this time you may experience profound changes of how you perceive, interpret and appreciate yourself and the world around you. Your relationships, both with yourself and with others, may enjoy new modes of expression and rise to new levels of understanding. The wisdom years are experienced between the ages of fifty-five and sixty-three.

During your wisdom cycle the 'how' of things is important to you, but the 'why' of things might be something you value even more. You are fully acquainted with the world. It is familiar to you. Yet, it may begin to dawn upon you that you know almost nothing at all. For instance, you may know 'how' the Sun passes through the skies each day, but you may be more interested to know 'why' the Sun does this. In other words, you may be familiar with the physics of life, but it is the metaphysics of life that now truly inspires you.

Your outlook on life might easily be dominated by the 'why' of things. This is true for all spheres of life. The success of your work, your relationships and your under-standing of the world will all be enhanced by any efforts you invest in the why of it all. As the German philosopher Friedrich Wilhelm Nietzsche once wrote, 'If we have our own why of life, we shall get along with almost any how.'

During your wisdom cycle you may discover that it is not what you want out of the world that is important to you, but rather what you understand of the world. The need to understand may be your motivation. Self-knowledge and self-understanding may open up new horizons of endeavour and expression. So too might knowledge and understanding of others and of the world around you. Understanding may well be your platform for living during this major life cycle.

Re-evaluation, a second opinion, a new appreciation and a new way of looking at life are all common experiences of the sixth major cycle of life. Perhaps the keynotes of this cycle are *meaning* and *appreciation*. Meaning often emerges from the attunement of appreciation—real appreciation. The more fully you live in tune with yourself and with the world around you, the more fully you will live in tune with the meaning of these things.

The time of your sixth cycle is also often a time for the appreciation of ideas and ideals. You may find that the ethics and morals of life are interesting to you. Art, music, poetry, literature and drama create stages for the enactment of ideas. These therefore may also be of interest to you. The spiritual and philosophical schools of teaching, training and conduct may also hold a new, or renewed, fascination.

Ideas and ideals may delight you, but you must make sure that this delight does not deteriorate into a realm of fantasy, wishes and idealism. Ideas and ideals hold their own power; they must be treated and cared for constructively. In other words, they should be employed in a practical sense. Otherwise there is a temptation to withdraw into a created world of ideals which has meaning only to you. Ideas and ideals are not dangerous; how you live with them may be.

During your wisdom cycle there are two years which are of particular interest and significance. The first is the year when you are fifty-five. This, in fact, is the first year of the wisdom cycle, and it is significantly influenced by two fives. This is interesting because you have just left your fifth major life cycle, where the power of five also dominated. We can conclude, therefore, that the power and potential of five is still very active at the beginning of your wisdom cycle. Thus, the meaning, understanding and appreciation specific to the wisdom cycle has a collective nature about it. The ancient history of a continent will hold a greater interest to you than the mechanics of a tin opener!

The other time of special significance and interest to the wisdom cycle is the last year of the cycle, when you will be sixty-three. The number sixty-three symbolizes the essential possible challenges or conflicts during this time. Six symbolizes the potential for spiritual and philosophical wisdom; three symbolizes the potential for rational and logical knowledge. Six embraces the intuitive; three embraces the intellectual. Six embodies the artistic; three embodies the practical. Six activates the psychic; three confines itself to the physical.

The potential conflicts between six and three are, therefore, apparent and obvious. However, there are subtleties involved. For instance, although the power of six in many ways transcends the power of three, six cannot live alone. Six needs the foundation of three to give it strength. For example, how can a person expect to contemplate the finer nature of things if he or she is not even able to concentrate well? Three empowers your ability to concentrate; six needs this power before it can operate through you safely or reliably.

Thus, the time of your sixth major life cycle gives you an opportunity to marry the power and potential of both the three and six. Your wisdom must be holistic—it must envelop the physical, emotional and mental, the will and the collective, leaving nothing out. Your wisdom must also embrace the creative, intuitive, psychic and spiritual—all of which are potential tools of wisdom and of meaning. Here, then, is the basis for gathering and imparting wisdom and meaning. Here, then, also, is the main challenge of this time.

Your Love Cycle

Your seventh major life cycle is the love cycle. This cycle holds a potential which may inspire the contemplative, the philosopher and the poet in you. Some of the key words for this most profound and evocative time are *contemplation*, *brotherhood*, *service*, *fusion* and *love*. Your love cycle lasts for nine years, from age sixty-four to seventy-two.

The wisdom of life inspires the philosophy of life. Therefore, your sixth major life cycle, the wisdom cycle, can be of great support to your seventh major life cycle, which is often characterized by philosophy, metaphysics and spirituality. The relationship between wisdom, philosophy and love is a precise, interdependent partnership. This relationship was aptly expressed by the nineteenth-century American poet, essayist and mystic Henry David Thoreau, who wrote, 'To be a philosopher is to love wisdom so as to live according to its dictates.'

One of the highest expressions of philosophy is love. Your seventh major life cycle is the cycle of love. To know, to express and to become love are the challenges of this particular cycle in your life. On the one hand, the word love refers to a devotion, a commitment, an attunement and a loyalty towards the object(s) of your love. On the other hand, the word love refers to a spiritual, unconditional, creative, inobtrusive relationship to something or someone.

In numerology the concept of Love has nine dimensions. There is the physical dimension of love, as governed by the number one. The lesson of one is to attune and devote yourself to physical growth and development. Then there is the emotional dimension of love, as governed by the number two, the lesson of which is to learn to feel and express love, and also to love and control your emotions. Next there is the mental dimension of love, as governed by the number three, in which you aim to experience and master mental love and commitment, mental devotion and attunement. One common mental manifestation of love is *concentration*.

The endeavour dimension of love is governed by the number four. The lesson of four is to learn to commit and endure, unconditionally. That which you love has a right to expect your support, loyalty and hard work. The collective dimension of love, as governed by the number five, teaches you how to give love impersonally, equally and to all. It is more important to know what it is you love about something or someone rather than what you dislike or hate. The wisdom dimension of love is governed by the number six. Here the lesson is to recognize, be attuned and love the wisdom of all things. Understanding facilitates love.

The love dimension of love is governed by the number seven. The lesson here is to love love, for the sake of love. Love deserves your devotion and your commitment. By radiating love we worship love, we begin to become love. There is also a spiritual dimension of love, as governed by the number eight. The spiritual expression of love is both the pursuit and the lesson of life. To respect and appreciate the spiritual in all things, to embrace the spiritual as best we can, and to attempt to live by the spiritual, amounts to a code and practice of spiritual love. The number nine governs the ninth dimension of love, the dimension of law. Love is the Law. *Work for love and love will work for you. Live by love and love will live by you.*

One of the highest expressions of love is *service*. During the time of your seventh major life cycle the emphasis is on brotherhood, community and service. When you follow your contemplations you will go deep within yourself; when you follow your aspirations you will reach out to the world through your actions. Devotion to unconditional service is one of the highest expressions of love. Your support for others will, subtly, be the support you find for yourself.

After love, after service, there comes *fusion*. Fusion describes that moment when you begin to relate to people and places as being linked to you and as being intimate parts of you. During the time of two you may have been tempted to grab and possess in order to find and keep love. Now, during the time of seven, you may find that by letting go and committing yourself to unconditional love you will discover a new octave and expression of love. Your concept of love has changed: *Give freedom, and you, naturally, hold on to love.*

In the seventh cycle of your life you may find you are a researcher and a communicator. You are exploring and relating things which may have been, up until now, completely new to you. The ability to live with love, in the fullest sense that you can give it, is perhaps the ultimate aim of this cycle. To be unconditional, to understand, to appreciate, to commit and attune yourself to life—these are also major themes for this time.

Your Spiritual Cycle

Your eighth major life cycle is the spiritual cycle. Its duration is nine years, beginning from the age of seventy-three up until and including the age of eighty-one. During this cycle the aims and lessons are, broadly speaking, to perceive the spiritual in all things, to appreciate and respect the spiritual in all things, and also to relate to the spiritual in all things. *Spiritual awareness* and *spiritual consciousness* light up your life during these years.

Your spiritual cycle can only be as strong as the other major cycles in your life. In particular, your spiritual cycle requires support from the collective cycle, in which collective consciousness begins to dawn; it requires the foundation of the wisdom cycle in which you learn to perceive, appreciate and relate to the wisdom in all things; and it requires the strength of the love cycle in which you learn to recognize, respect and communicate with the love in all things. In truth, though, the strength of any major cycle of your life is dependent upon the strength of *each and every* major life cycle. This is a spiritual truth.

During your spiritual cycle the awareness that you are a spiritual being is of paramount importance. The essence of you is spiritual. The essence of all people is spiritual. Living during the time of eight is to live with the essential in all people and of all things. There is a beautiful saying from the Sufi tradition which confirms what is said here. It reads, 'To treat every human being as a shrine of God is to fulfil all religion.'

Spiritual living is the essential aim of your spiritual cycle. This is a time to seek and to search, to question and to discover, to tie up or to unfold, and to embrace, finally, once and for all, your spiritual existence. If you have not had a spiritual philosophy until now, this might be the most surprising, exciting and revealing time of your life. If before now you have lived with a spiritual awareness, now is the time to turn that living awareness into an ever greater living conviction.

One of the highest truths of numerology is that every number has a spiritual potential, and also that every cycle of your life, major and minor, has a spiritual potential.

Therefore, a very useful exercise to do during the time of your Spiritual Cycle, or at any time in your life, is to look at your life—past, present and future—and attempt to spiritualize whatever it is you focus on. There is a spiritual lesson and teaching in all your experiences, if you look for it.

To spiritualize the potential of the number one, you may like to contemplate the idea that the human race is the expression of One Intelligence, One Being. To spiritualize the power of the number two, you may like to contemplate the truth that every human being is an expression of both matter and spirit. To spiritualize the possibilities of number three, you may like to contemplate the trinity—a worldwide, multi-faith concept—and also on the spiritual potential of the brain and of thought.

To spiritualize the potential of the number four, you may like to contemplate the spiritual potential of will, work and endeavour. To what can you give your support? What monument will you build? You may also like to contemplate the cross. To activate the spiritual potential of the number five, you may like to contemplate your unique place in and contribution to the collective scheme of life. To tap the spiritual potential of the number six, light up the wisdom star and let this be your guiding light in all that you perceive.

To contact the spiritual potential of the number seven, explore, experience and play with the all-pervasive power of love. Love is an energy you can control and manipulate for the benefit of yourself and others. To experience the spiritual potential of the number eight, reach inwards and upwards, and allow yourself to become a channel for spiritual expression, *in all things*. And, to enjoy the spiritual potential of the number nine, learn to perceive, discriminate and encounter the spiritual truth in all things.

During the time of eight it is good to be conscious of

being a channel for expression and inspiration outside of yourself. For so much of your life you may have relied upon your own personal reserves of inspiration (and of perspiration!) for support. Now is the time, then, to attempt to open yourself up to the space that is beyond you, and to allow for ideas to flow through you. For so much of your life you may have put all of yourself into your endeavours. Now is a time, then, to put as little of yourself into a project as possible, and to see what comes through.

The essential challenge of your spiritual cycle revolves around the relationship between the number eight and its shadow number one. At the age of eighteen, the one is the primary number and the eight the secondary; at age eighty-one it is the eight that is the primary number and one the secondary. The eight should lead. If it does not you risk denying yourself the spiritual experiences of life during this time. The grip of the number one can become so firm that spiritual experience, expression and realization can all be denied throughout a person's entire life.

Now is the time to let go of the fear of the unknown. Now is the time to die to the material life and be reborn into the spiritual life. Now is the time to enjoy and play with the possibilities of intuitive, psychic, creative and healing expression. Activating the spiritual potential within you is a perfect preparation for every day of your life. It is also the perfect preparation for death, transition and change. *Spiritual living brings with it its own reward, which is spiritual living*.

Your Law Cycle

Your ninth major life cycle is governed by the number nine. It is the cycle of law, and occurs over the nine years that rest between the first day of eighty-two and the final day of ninety. Nine is the numerological symbol of *perception* and *discrimination*. It is also the symbol for *judgement* and *truth*, for *completion* and *conclusion*. As such, these are the main themes of your final major life cycle.

The number nine is a great teacher. Traditionally nine is linked with our *Higher Self*, that inner part of our being which is already perfect. Its potential, its message, is that *life is a university and the experiences of life are lessons*. There is an understanding to be gained from every experience and perception we have. This includes numbers. The number one brings with it its lessons. The numbers two, three, four, five, and so on, all have lessons. *Ignore the lesson; forgo the teaching*.

One of the keynotes of the time of nine is to watch for the lesson in all things. The people you meet, the places you go, your successes, failures, disappointments, surprises—they all carry a lesson. Wherever, whenever, whatever, whoever, if you take the time, there is, under-pinned, a lesson which motivates and supports the experi-ence. Number nine is the watcher; it reminds us that this is so.

The potential of nine promotes a desire to know the truth of the world. It teaches us to watch, see and perceive the truth of all things. The lesson of experience is bound up in the truth of it. Therefore, learning to discriminate between black and white, right and wrong, true and false—these are some of the lessons of nine. What is the truth of your life? What are the lessons still to be learned? These are the sorts of questions that the potential of nine can provoke within you.

Fair, objective judgement is another of the ideals of nine. The ninth cycle is positioned very purposefully in your life. This cycle offers you the ideal opportunity to practise self-judgement so as to learn and grow. Self-judgement should not be reserved only for this cycle, however. The minor cycles of days, months and years, and the personal birthdate numbers and personal name numbers often carry the nine potential. Thus, the potential of nine is with you for all of your life, and on certain days, months and years it is with you especially. It is never too soon or too late to tap the potential of nine—the opportunities of nine are everywhere and always.

Reviewing a life requires skill. It is a delicate affair. The object of self-judgement is to help you to grow, not to suffer. Hindsight and retrogression make life look easy. Yes, there are lessons for you still to learn. Yes, some have and some have not been learned. Take time to assess what it is you could do and should do, now. During the ninth life cycle it is true that your life is coming to an end, but that does not mean to say that the lessons will stop.

The time of nine also offers you the chance and the opportunity, *if you will take it*, to clear up any unfinished business. Now is the time to complete and to conclude. This is particularly true around the age of ninety, which promotes the influence of nine, the symbol of completion, and the influence of zero, the symbol for the time before the beginning of new life. In other words, the ninth cycle may be offering you your last chance to patch up and clear up, to complete and to fulfil.

Unsatisfactory endings cannot be healed so easily as unsatisfactory beginnings. Satisfactory endings are rare. They elude us, most often because the lesson eludes us. Now is the time to be wise, as may be experienced during the time of six. Now is the time to love and forgive, as may be experienced during the time of seven. Now is the time to recognize and keep to the spiritual, as may be experienced during the time of eight. Now, during the cycle of nine, is the time to absorb the lessons of life, and thereby write your own ending.

CHAPTER SIX

THE NUMEROLOGICAL YEAR

Timeliness is best in all matters.

Hesiod, Works and Days (eighth century BC)

The numerologist aims to live in harmony with the cycles of space and time that are operating both around and within him or her. To live in harmony with both the world around you and the world within you is considered to be one of the highest forms of healing. It is also considered in numerology to be a mark of adeptness, mastery and enlightenment.

There is a precise time and moment for each and every plan and action. The success of a thought, idea or project depends much upon our attunement to and co-ordination with time. The right time is a kind of magic, for, as the numerologist believes, anything can be achieved if the time be right. If the time is wrong, no matter how good the endeavour or intention might be, it is surely doomed to failure. This idea is reflected in the Persian proverb, 'A stone thrown at the right time does better than gold given at the wrong time.'

The belief that there is a time for everything and that all things have their time is expressed nowhere more beautifully than in the poetic lines of Ecclesiastes (3: 1–8). This following passage is a profound and evocative contemplation of the nature of time and our relationship with it. It begins,

To every thing there is a season, and a time to every purpose under heaven:
A time to be born, and a time to die; a time to plant, and a time to pluck up that which is planted;
A time to kill, and a time to heal; a time to break down, and a time to build up;
A time to weep, and a time to laugh; a time to mourn, and a time to dance;
A time to cast away stones, and a time to gather stones together; a time to embrace, and a time to refrain from embracing;
A time to get and a time to lose; a time to keep, and a time to cast away;
A time to rend, and a time to sew; a time to keep silence, and a time to speak;
A time to love, and a time to hate; a time of war, and a time of peace.

Some of us know instinctively when the time is right to perform a certain action. Our intuition, or inner voice, or unconscious prompting—call it what you will—guides us in such a way that we plan and act in harmony with the right time and place. In ancient times numerology schools would encourage this intuitive faculty through an understanding of the science and philosophy of numbers. There is, they believed, *a season, and a time to every purpose under heaven.*

The Universal Year

The number of the *Universal Year* represents the possible potential in the world that exists around you for that year. Every year, therefore, has a universal number and a universal potential which is available to and affects each of us to some degree. *The life of a Universal Year is encoded in the life of its universal number.*

Numerology states that the space around you is not empty. On the contrary it is vibrant, alive and filled with possibilities. You live in a sea of free-flowing energy and potential. It is possible to tap into this potential if you so attune yourself and the moment is right. How exciting it is to see that modern mathematical physics also now holds the view that space is neither empty nor lifeless.

To calculate the universal number of a Universal Year, you simply add together the four primary integers of the year. For example:

UNIVERSAL YEAR CHART FOR THE 1990s:

$$1990 = 1 + 9 + 9 + 0 = 19 = 1$$
$$1991 = 1 + 9 + 9 + 1 = 20 = 2$$
$$1992 = 1 + 9 + 9 + 2 = 21 = 3$$
$$1993 = 1 + 9 + 9 + 3 = 22 = 4$$
$$1994 = 1 + 9 + 9 + 4 = 23 = 5$$
$$1995 = 1 + 9 + 9 + 5 = 24 = 6$$
$$1996 = 1 + 9 + 9 + 6 = 25 = 7$$
$$1997 = 1 + 9 + 9 + 7 = 26 = 8$$
$$1998 = 1 + 9 + 9 + 8 = 27 = 9$$
$$1999 = 1 + 9 + 9 + 9 = 28 = 1$$

The universal number is a symbol for a part of the universal potential of any given year. It is highly significant and influential, but it is not the only number at work. On one level, the universal number is all you need to know about a Universal Year. However, if you care to dig a little deeper, there are one or two interesting points to be made about the Universal Year Chart for the 1990s.

The first point of interest is the unusually high occurrence of the power of nine. Whenever the nine predominates, the Higher Law, decision, research and discrimination are thought to be particularly operative. From 1991 to 1998 there are two nines active in the Universal Year. The power of two is also a power of decision and discrimination, operating mainly on the feminine, intuitive, sensitive and soulful levels. Therefore, in terms of the Universal Year the 1990s are a time in which to research, operate with, discriminate with, decide in accordance with and listen to our feminine intuition, feeling and soulful level.

The second point of interest is that the Universal Years from 1990 to 1998 travel through the second major life cycle of emotion and intuition (19–27). Thus, once again, the feminine powers of intuition, feeling and soulfulness are particularly abundant during the decade of the 90s. It is also interesting to note that the year 2000 will be the first time in a thousand years that the physical power of the number one will not be influential. In the next millennium the feminine power of two will be ever-present.

If we look around our world, there is plenty of evidence to suggest a transformation from the masculine, physical power of one to the more feminine, soulful power of two. Society is now beginning to empower women and the status of womanhood. Men are gradually becoming aware of and opening up to their feminine (anima, yang) qualities. Physics—with the advent of the quantum, holistic approaches, as opposed to the mechanistic, reductionist approaches—has discovered the poetic.

Medicine is becoming an art again, with the coming of complementary medicines such as healing, drama, art and dance therapies, aromatherapy, massage and so on. There are movements in religion which are reacting against the tight structural and theological dogma of the churches.

Surely, the increase in the practical, intuitive Eastern and Oriental schools and philosophies is also evidence of a new thirst and a new appetite.

Perhaps this all has something to do with the new element of two that is in the air?

The Personal Year

The number of your *Personal Year* represents potential and possibilities particular to you and your own individual cycles of existence. Instead of relating to the potential and possibilities around you, as the *Universal Year Number* does, the *Personal Year Number* relates to the potential and possibilities that are generated within you. Therefore, you must look outwards to discover the powers that are operating through a Universal Year, and inwards to discover the powers that are operating through your Personal Year.

The way of numerology is a journey to the Self. It advocates constant self-analysis, inspires self-discovery, and hopefully thereby promotes and supports self-realization. Numerology professes to be a scientific and philosophical system of personal growth. The numbers which make up a person's numerological chart are signposts, clues, guidelines, directions and signals, all of which may inspire wisdom, growth and harmony.

To arrive at your own personal year number, you add the day of your birth to the month of your birth and then to the number of the current Universal Year. To illustrate this, let us take the example of the British actor and filmmaker Charlie Chaplin. Charlie Chaplin was born in 1889. The universal year number for that year would have been $1 + 8 + 8 + 9 = 26 = 8$. It is interesting to note that some of the common trademarks of eight are communication, creativity and success. As an artist of mime, Charlie Chaplin was unparalleled.

If Charlie Chaplin were alive in 1992, his personal year number would be five. This figure is arrived at like so:

Date of Birth	+	Month of Birth	+	Universal Year
16 = 7		4 (April)		21 (1 + 9 + 9 + 2) = 3

Personal Year Number = 7 + 4 + 3 = 14 = 5

As it happened, Charlie Chaplin died in 1977. That year, his personal year number was an eight. It is very interesting to note that the number eight has a strong link with Spirit, and therefore with death or transition from matter to Spirit. As previously stated in Chapter 5, many people pass on in an eight cycle of life. Charlie Chaplin was in an eight cycle when he died. This observation does not prove a law, only a tendency. Numerology does not deal in dogma, only in potential, possibilities and probabilities. It just so happens that the pull of Spirit during a cycle of eight is stronger than at most other times, and therefore the initiation of death is often quite likely.

Personal and Universal Year Numbers

Influences and Potentials

This following section gives you a quick reference guide to influences, potentials, possibilities and probabilities that may be operating during any given yearly cycle. Just as it is good and wise to attune yourself to the different seasons of the year, as is still taught in the Chinese Shen cycles of Fire, Earth, Metal, Water and Wood, for instance, so too is it good and wise to attune yourself to the universal and personal potential of a given year.

Once you have determined the universal year number, and also your personal year number, it is interesting to compare and contrast the influences, potentials, possibilities and probabilities associated with these two numbers. For instance, if in the same year both the universal year number and your personal year number is one, then you may experience a very potent time for beginnings, enterprise and making an impact.

If, on the other hand, the universal year number is seven and your personal year number is two, then you may find you are engaging in a struggle between emotions and love, separation and unity, and so on. Which potential and power will you side with, align yourself to, and call upon? To take a further example, if the universal year number is four and your personal year number is five, you may find you will have to make choices between what is good for you and what is good for others. Which direction will you take? Which direction should you take? And which potential will you tap into?

If in the same year the universal year number is six and your personal year number is three, then logic must support your wisdom, but not overshadow it. The skills of the knowledgeable person and the skills of the wise person can support each other, but these potentials are very different. Once again, as always, the choice as to what potential you tap into is yours. Which wave will you ride? We are back again at synchronicity and working in harmony with the energies around you and within you. This is numerology.

According to your own individual arrangement of numbers, you will find from time to time that your personal birthdate number is the same as and therefore synchronizes with another number, such as your personal year number, the universal year number, your personal month number, the universal month number, your personal day number, or the universal day number. Rarely is there an easier, better time to tap into a potential. With synchronicity you do not need to reach out for it so much as simply allow it to flow through you. These special, pregnant occasions happen on only a handful of occasions in our lives. We must be careful not to miss them!

One: A Good Time to Start
This is an excellent time for watching out for and embarking on new ventures, associations and enterprises. This applies to work and occupations but also to relationships and friendships. New people in your life, or old friends who make a fresh impact, are common at this time. This can also be a time for re-commitment, re-beginnings and re-birth.

The power of one is a power of energy, dynamism and activity. Many things will be happening around you. Opportunity, fresh pastures, a new job, new hobbies, or moving house are all common occurrences. The challenge of the time of one is to face up to new opportunities and change with confidence and optimism, and not to shy away from it all through fear and uncertainty. The Universe provides opportunity; you, in turn, must provide the courage and the wisdom to know when, how and with what to act.

During the time of one it is important to attend to number one. Self-analysis, self-knowledge and self-realization are all keynotes of the potential symbolized by the number one. Learning to assert and express yourself may also be part of the agenda for this year. Dig deep, and look well into yourself. Who are you? To what do you truly aspire? Where are you going?

Mentally you may be easily inspired by creative and

original thought and ideas. This can be a time to contemplate a change of direction, or a re-dedication on a course you have already set. You must set your stall out during this time, and therefore goal-setting, direction and a well-laid path for your life must all be attended to.

Success, or at least the promise of success, often comes easily during the time of one. However, do not be content merely with success. It is essential that you choose your success, and that not just any old success chooses you. Beware of the temptation to stay superficial and shallow during the time of one. Haste, impetuosity, impatience and innocence may all play their hand.

Courage, confidence, determination and vision are also part of the potential and power of one. You can call upon these potentials to help you challenge, probe and go beyond mere physical and material successes. The rewards in the long run will be fuller and longer lasting. One more note of caution: compete with yourself and no one else. In truth, *the greatest competition of all lies within you*.

Two: Review, Revise and Consolidate

During the time of two it can be very good to review and revise, and also to strengthen and consolidate any actions or beginnings you may have undertaken during the time of one. You have made a good start; now it is time to maintain the rhythm and keep you and your enterprise on course. Like a good wine, ideas and enterprises mature with time. Beware that the powers, energies and ideas generated during the time of one are not dispersed or dissipated unnecessarily during the time of two.

This is also a time to co-operate with others. Look around you and see to what you can give support, and by what you can be supported. Your connections with and to the people in your life are also highly significant at this time. The time of two invokes the intuitive and the feminine, and also touches upon feeling and soul levels. Therefore, your relationships can lead you to deeper, stronger and more meaningful levels and dimensions of happiness and fulfilment.

The potential of two can certainly incorporate co-operation and union. On the other hand, it can also involve competition and division, disaster and strife—and nowhere is this more significant than within our own selves. The time of two is often regarded in numerological traditions as a power of ill fortune. This is because two is often linked to duality and division, from which there can spring unrest, disharmony and disorder.

During the time of two it can be very important to watch the play of your emotions and feelings. When you are motivated, inspired or compelled to do something, know what it is that is driving you. Beware of emotional haste and mental uncertainty. Inaction, delay and allowing time to pass can be very practical remedies for indecision. Thought and contemplation are as important as action and endeavour during the time of two.

On a more positive note, the power of two can often invoke the feminine, intuitive and creative potentials of our nature. Relaxation, contemplation and meditation may help you to tap into and develop this potential even further. Listen to your inner voice. Learn to understand and then trust your intuition. Face up to the feminine. This can also be a very soulful time, during which you make great inroads and achievements with your own personal relationship with yourself.

Three: Go for Go

A year of three can often be a time for the blossoming of actions and ideas, partnerships and relationships. The time of three is usually one of advance, development, progression and achievement. It is also often associated with luck, coincidence, destiny and fate. If you apply yourself well during this time you will attract the forces of luck, coincidence, destiny and fate that you deserve.

The time of three is considered, after the time of one, to be the next best time for beginnings and starting something new. In particular the power of three is thought to promote mental breakthroughs, and also to inspire intellectual ideas, theories and aspirations. If the year of one is a time of action and the year of two is a time of nurturing and support, then, the year of three is a time of thought, conjecture, mentation, head- and brain-work. Be sure, though, that you do not only practise abstract intellectual exercises. Practical application of your theories is vital.

The year of three can often present new opportunity and interest socially. The potential of three has a dynamic, optimistic and extrovert dimension to it, and therefore the time of three often allows a person to shine in public and in the social arena. New friendships, acquaintances, contacts and connections are very common during the time of three. A new-found appreciation, respect and interest in current and old friends and relations can also emerge. The time of three can certainly be a very rewarding time for social interest.

It can be very common during the time of three for the outward gaze to be so strong that you can forget to attend to your inner self. Mental preoccupation and overload can mean that you forget your physical and emotional health and well-being. More importantly, you can also forget to nourish your spirit. We must ensure that we are at least prepared to hop down from our mental perch from time to time, particularly during any major period of three.

On a more positive note, mental churnings can lead to high inspiration and creative, original output. Trust your creative nature, hold back the critic, judge and jury and allow yourself to receive inspiration, guidance and new ideas. You have a vast mental reservoir of potential which can easily be activated by the three potential, and also by its shadow number six.

The more you attend to your inner space during the time of three the more you may be able to tap into the power of six and its potential for wisdom. This can happen if you are prepared to return again and again to the All-Knowledge Space within you, and if you are prepared to transcend and go beyond that which you already know and are familiar with. Mental exploration and the discovery of a treasure chest of wisdom are all part of the potential of the time of three.

Four: Keep Your Eye on the Shovel

A year of four is a good time for productive and satisfying work. Application, attention to detail and disciplined persistence can all help to yield desired results. This is a time for earthing ideas which have manifested in earlier years, for making them concrete, more solid and secure.

In relationships, the time of four is all about strengthening commitments to the people in your life, and working hard to ensure that the quality of these commitments is all that you want it to be. It is also all about getting involved with life and with the people around you. Get stuck in. Positive action, persistent effort and sustained endeavour are the keynotes for this time, and the more effort and application you put into the time of four the greater your rewards will be. Perspiration earns inspiration!

Your resources are endless. Your potential is unlimited. Your willpower will amaze you. The only limits in your life are those you set yourself. By tapping into the power of four, you can take on the strength, courage and bravery to 'boldly go where no [person] has gone before'! All it takes is a belief in your ability to work both hard and well.

The power of four is a building energy, and therefore the time of four provides opportunity for self-improvement and for building up your feelings of self-worth, -esteem and -assurance. Attending to your own self, working with your emotions, strengthening your mind and feeding the spiritual are also all part of the work potential of four. Be sure not to miss out any level. Attend to them all, for they are all a part of you.

One note of caution: once you activate your willpower you must learn to use it appropriately, and to ensure that you control it and that it does not control you. You will be strong and you will be powerful. Do not abuse this. Also, do not forget to spend time away from the grind. Remember, from time to time, the fruits of rest, relaxation, the arts, play, a holiday, a good meal, friendships, social engagements and anything else that supports enjoyment for enjoyment's sake.

Five: All Change

The time of five can often herald new horizons, fresh pastures and an expansion of possibilities and probabilities on every level. It is a time for a major shift in priorities, directions and emphasis. Your relationship to your work, partners, friends and the whole wide world may take on a new order and meaning. The time of five is thus, potentially, a time of change.

Opening up to the potential of five demands bravery and faith. Whereas it is you who generates the powers of one, two, three and four, the powers of five, six, seven, eight and nine are generated through you. The first four years in a nine-year cycle place an overt, outer emphasis on the individual: year one emphasizes the physical self, year two the emotional self, year three the mental self and year four the individual will. Year five, however, places a covert, inner emphasis on the collective will and on the greater, higher ambition and will of humanity.

Thus, if you allow yourself to open up to the influence and potential of five, your perceptions and perspectives must change, and they often do so radically. Instead of perceiving yourself as an individual citizen of a world, you may now begin to perceive yourself as a world citizen belonging to and living in harmony with a single order.

Your ideas and work, instead of being motivated by your own petty individual ego, may now expand so as to embrace greater, collective benefits and ideals. Meaning and purpose can often be essential to you from now on. If you have been working with small ideas and groups up to now, you may begin to work with bigger ideas, in grander arenas.

It is as if you have been happy travelling along in fourth gear for some time and have only just remembered now that you also have a fifth gear. Now the ride will be smoother and more economical. Unlike in the year of four, hard work, disciplined application and sustained endeavour are not the order of the day. On the contrary, now is the time to relax, to give yourself permission to open up to ideas, plans and designs, many of which may feel bigger than you. Effective communication is certainly a keynote of five.

The philosopher within you may begin to stir during the time of five. Satisfying your own individual needs, dreams and desires may no longer be enough. Your own world, comfortable and rewarding to you for so long, may now not be satisfactory. Now might be a time to sacrifice your own ambitions and to align yourself to a greater project or need. All this is certainly part of the potential of five.

The traveller within you may also begin to stir during the time of five. New horizons may also include new cultures, civilizations and cities to visit or even settle down in. If you open up to the power of five, and also resist the temptation to fall back on the shadow power of four, then you may well be empowered by a desire to travel, explore and discover.

The time of five is certainly a time of change. The change usually happens from within and then manifests out and around you. Therefore, the need to travel within yourself and to explore and discover more about yourself is also very important during the time of five. Inner promptings may well challenge your status quo.

The challenge of five is not merely to change, but to make the right change. The year of five can easily become a struggle for influence and control between the powers of four and five. You have lived through a year of four, and now, in the year of five, your shadow power is a four. If you fall back upon four now you may well be denying yourself. Now is a time to open yourself up, to go beyond yourself and put your faith in a greater cause than your own good self!

Six: Be Wise

The year of six is a time to be really wise about all that has passed in your life, a time to recognize and learn from all the lessons of the present, and also a time to plan for the future in a cool, wise fashion. Wisdom is your keynote during the time of six. We all have the capacity to be wise and skilful, and now is the time to tap into that innate potential.

During the time of six, both the potential of six and its shadow power, three, are at play. Six represents wisdom and knowing, whereas three represents reason and intellect. The subtle differences of six and three were perfectly expressed by the first Archbishop of Canterbury, St Augustine, who in his fifth-century work *On the Trinity* wrote, 'To wisdom belongs the intellectual apprehension of eternal things; to knowledge the rational knowledge of temporal things.' Rest with these words for a while.

The difference between three and six may also be found in the words of the English poet William Cowper, who in *Winter Walk at Noon* contemplated that, 'Knowledge is proud that he has learned so much; Wisdom is humble that he knows no more.' Six stands on a higher octave than three. It is at once supported by and transcends three. Three represents mental activity, dexterity and cleverness. Six is an experience, an inner knowing and way of being.

During the time of six it is good to sink below life's superficial gloss and there tarry a while so as to probe, observe and listen to the designs, drives and ambitions that motivate and inspire the events of the surface. It is also a good idea, during this time, to transcend and fly, hover over and observe the surface distractions of life.

Think before you act, at all times. One of the traits of a truly wise person is that he or she does not give way to desperation. Try to train yourself to stay cool, calm and centred at all times. Deep within you there is an All-Knowledge Space which, when you are still, quiet and poised, can inspire and guide you. The voice of your intuition will counsel you. Rest with the three only and you run the risk of turning off the light of six.

The time of six can present a good opportunity to indulge yourself in beauty. Look for, appreciate and be thankful for the beauty there is around you. This can be a time to call the creative impulses within you to the surface. The year of six can also be a time to awaken the communicator within you. Recognize and take advantage of the chance to communicate wisdom, beauty and creativity where possible. Let these principles be your guiding lights.

As well as stirring the poet in you, the potential of six may also arouse the romantic. One of the challenges and rewards of six is to appreciate, appraise and applaud that which you value in life. As the American poet and essayist Emerson once wrote, 'Life is a festival only to the wise.' Celebrate life! Recognize, relish and respond to the finer qualities of life. Aim to become at one with that which resonates with you.

Seven: Contemplate

The year of seven may present an excellent opportunity for spiritual focus, study and growth. The birth of spiritual awareness, appetite and endeavour are all potentials associated with the number seven. If you be brave enough you will allow yourself to open up to your spiritual dimension. Up until now you may have neglected or avoided the spiritual. Now, then, is the time to search for the spiritual, to learn its language and also to face up to and embrace it.

When in the year of seven, you need look no further than to the poetic inspiration of writer Richard Wilbur for guidance and direction. In *Advice to a Prophet* there is a passage which goes, 'Teach me, like you, to drink creation whole; And, casting out my self, become a soul.' Nowhere is the challenge of seven more aptly expressed. The lessons of seven are all lessons of the soul.

The time of seven can be a time for love in all of its highest expressions and manifestations. It can be, in particular, a time for being truly generous in all your actions. Learning to give and to receive unconditional love is essential. Love without reward, love as a result of wisdom and knowing, and love for love's sake are all keynotes of the number seven.

The potential of seven is quite clearly on a higher octave than its shadow power of two. One of the challenges of the time of seven is to go beyond the two and invoke the seven potential. The year of seven can therefore be a time of emotional unrest and indecision. Pain is a signal for disturbance and sickness; it can also, though, be a signal of healing and growth. You should embrace the potential of two, but not if it means it will eclipse the potential of seven.

Relationships will alter during the time of seven. The most satisfying relationships are those which support each individual's rights to creativity, freedom and personal growth. Emotional instability can sometimes deny these rights. The potential of seven provides the strength and determination to move beyond this instability. Giving one another freedom is no longer perceived as a risk. In fact, it is a compliment that becomes a necessity.

The ability to attune yourself to others, to become one with another person's feelings and also to fuse and connect with those people, spaces and environments around you, may manifest and heighten during the time of seven. You may begin to experience yourself as more at one with yourself and also more at one with the world you perceive and experience.

Eight: Connect

The year of eight is a time to contact, resonate and network with others. It is a time to interconnect and intercommunicate, so that your own individual energy and movement merges and becomes part of a greater task. Making a connection with yourself, resonating and living in tune with yourself, can also be a potential and possibility for the time of eight. Indeed, it can be a time to make connections on every level of your life.

The power of one can help you recognize your potential to become a unique, creative and adventurous individual. The power of eight can help you recognize your uniqueness, also. In particular it helps you recognize your spiritual originality. It also teaches that your distinctiveness does not isolate you from humanity. On the contrary, it connects you to humanity. All of humanity is within you, and all of you is a part of humanity. One of the essential differences between one and eight is that one inspires material ambition and success while eight inspires spiritual ambition and success.

Looking for the essential, be it in business plans, people or ideas, is one of the challenges commonly experienced during the year of eight. That which appears on the surface is not always a faithful reflection of that which lies beneath or above it. The ability to observe, see, witness and look into the life ahead, and into the people who are a part of your life, is an essential attribute throughout this year. The more you connect to the essence of what you do and what or whom you are interested in, the greater success you can experience.

The year of eight is often a time to practise solitude, silence and quiet. Once again, as with every number, the events of your own inner world are just as significant as those events that happen around you in your everyday life. The emphasis here is again connection to yourself. Practising the art of being centred, of calm and coolness in your everyday life, will be very beneficial to you.

Eight can be a time when we witness death. We all know about physical death, but this is not the only kind of death there is. Sometimes death might mean the death of past instability, failings and weaknesses. The caterpillar dies in order to experience flight and freedom as a butterfly. We must be prepared to shed old skins if they no longer serve us well. There will be times in your life when you outgrow yourself and others; at that time you must be prepared to move on.

Whereas the power of one activates masculine strength and success, the power of eight activates feminine strength and success. Your intuitive, creative and psychic self may, therefore, begin to flower or develop more deeply during the time of eight. The intuitive, creative and psychic dimensions of your Self are intangible, invisible and hard to measure or assess, especially at first. This does not mean we should disown them.

The time of eight can also be a time to give and receive support. Those people who are close to you and with whom you connect will appreciate your strength, commitment and support. There may well also be times when you will be grateful to them for their efforts and for their presence. We are unique and we are individuals, but, as John Donne wrote, 'No man is an island.' Indeed, *No man can be an island*.

Nine: Finish

The year of nine takes you to the end of a natural cycle in life. It is not, therefore, the time for new beginnings or starting afresh. Rather, it is a time to review and revise, to measure and assess. Look into the past and determine what went well, what went wrong—and then ask why. Every year is a special year; and every year has great importance. This is particularly true of any nine year. The more thorough and conscientious you are during the time of nine, the smoother will be your passage during the next cycle.

During the time of nine it is good to reflect upon and contemplate the events of the previous eight years. One of the greatest lessons of life is that there are always lessons to be learned. Look to each of the previous years and assess what you learned and what you have still to learn; look to where you triumphed and where you may have failed. Self-analysis in every department of your life will strengthen your resolve and serve you well in your future cycles of experience.

The time of nine can be the greatest of all. It is during the nine year that you may enjoy the fruits, rewards and culminations of your efforts in each of the previous eight years. This is the time for completion, climax, peaks, summits, and the final word. Prepare yourself to be a receiver, and give yourself permission to receive. This is essential preparation for your future cycles.

If life can be likened to a spiralling staircase reaching up to the sky, then when you reach a nine year you have climbed and completed another level of that staircase and must now prepare to approach a new landing and a new level of experience. You will be armed with the promise of potential within you and before you, and also with the lessons and experience of the past.

Now is also the time to finish, conclude and close the affairs of the past. It is a time to create balance, both within you and around you. If you are still owed, now is the time to allow yourself to receive; if you are still owing, then now is the time to ensure that you settle up. Look to friends, relationships, business, the spiritual, and every other area of your life, and determine how you can best balance and settle up. Unfinished business must now be concluded.

Honesty and fairness, both to yourself and to others, are keynotes for the time of nine. The more honest and fair you are now, both to yourself and to others, the more honest and fair life will be to you during the next cycle. Self-judgement is vital. It is also vital to be neither too hard nor too lenient with yourself. This would defeat the object of both numerology and life, which is the growth and development of your potential, and thereby the discovery and realization of your true nature.

CHAPTER SEVEN

THE NUMEROLOGICAL
CALENDAR MONTH

Each day the world is born anew,
For him who takes it rightly.

James Russell Lowell

Among the most exciting challenges of life are the abilities
to recognize, appreciate and capture the opportunities that
are unique to each and every day. It is as if each day
uncovers a fresh map of uncharted territory, and that
within each and every map there is a buried treasure. Each
day offers, therefore, potential, possibilities and probabilities—many of which might never sail by your way
again.

To live in the present is a present in itself. It is in the
moment of *Now* that we can be powerful, take control and
make changes. With the past, we recall, remember and
reflect; with the future, we hope, prepare and anticipate.
So often both the past and future have such a hold on us
that we avoid, neglect or maybe forget to recognize,
appreciate and capture the moment of *Now*. And yet, *it is
in the Now that we can create both the past and the future that we
desire.*

It is in the *Now*, when we live for the moment, that we
can tune in and tap into the potentials which, at that very

moment, are alive both within us and around us. Each day, if we can allow ourselves to be *born anew*, we can enrich ourselves and others by this heightened sense of appreciation for life and for living. To experience each day as a full single life in itself is one of the ideal aims of numerology. To live in tune with the potential of the moment, to synchronize with the thought of the moment, and to co-operate with the action of the moment, are all expressions of this ideal aim.

The numerologist studies the philosophy and science of numbers to become attuned to and help synchronize the rhythms and cycles of potential and opportunity operating during any given moment. By contemplating the meaning of each number, it is possible to live with an awareness which is wholly appropriate to each particular moment of your life. Therefore, not only does each year have a number, but also each month and each day. Indeed, if you know the exact minute and second of your birth you can also calculate the numbers for every minute and second of your life. This might be taking things a bit far, though!

As always, there are two rhythms and cycles operating during any moment. One is the universal rhythm and cycle, which supports all life. This pattern refers mostly to the life and potential that is around you. The other is the personal rhythm and cycle, which is unique to you. This pattern refers mostly to the life and potential that is within you.

Your Universal Month Number

Every month in your life represents a cycle in time which has both universal potentials and personal potentials —*potentials that are particular to that time*. These potentials are symbolized by a *universal number* and a *personal number*, respectively.

A simple and very powerful practice of numerology is that, at the beginning of a new monthly cycle, you should sit down and contemplate the meaning of your universal month number. In this way you can train yourself to synchronize and attune yourself to the surrounding potential of the moment.

Arriving at your universal month number is a relatively straightforward calculation. You simply add the current universal year number to the current calendar month, the sum of which is the universal month number.

Universal Year	+	Calendar Month	=	Universal Month

This calculation is best illustrated by an example. Therefore, let us take the date **1st January 1993**. First you must arrive at the universal year number. To do this you add all the numbers of the year, 1993, the sum of which will be the universal year number: $1 + 9 + 9 + 3 = 22$. To arrive at a single integer for the universal year number you then add $2 + 2$ (22) to arrive at **4**. Four is the universal year number for 1993.

The number of the month of **January** is one. Therefore, to arrive at the universal calendar month number, you now add 4 ($1 + 9 + 9 + 3$) to 1 (January) to arrive at **5**. Five is the universal month number for January 1993. Therefore, the five potential will be active on a universal dimension during this time. You would be very wise, therefore, at the beginning of a month of five to take time to contemplate, for instance, your place in and possible contribution to the progress of humanity.

Your Personal Month Number

It is also a very good practice of numerology that, at the beginning of each new monthly cycle, you take time to contemplate the possible potential and opportunities that are symbolized by your personal month number. While the universal month number is a symbol for the life around you, your personal month number is a symbol for the life within you. Therefore, contemplating your personal month number requires more introspection and internal reflection.

Your universal numbers always ask you to look, watch and study the world around you; your personal numbers, on the other hand, always ask you to adopt an inward gaze—to look, watch and study the world that bubbles up from within you. *To look out and to look in*, at whatever it is you are experiencing, is part of the fundamental purpose and lesson of numerology.

To arrive at your personal month number, you simply add your current personal year number to your current calendar month number, the sum of which is your personal month number.

Personal Year	+	Calendar Month	=	Personal Month

To illustrate this calculation by example, we shall assume that your personal year number has already been arrived at. The full equation for this number is given in Chapter 6. Therefore, we shall assume that your personal year number is seven. We can then take a calendar month, such as February, the number for which is two. To arrive at your personal month number, you add 7 + 2 (personal year number + number for February) to arrive at **9**. Nine is the personal month number. During this time you would be very wise indeed to look to the lessons and the truths in your life, and also to discriminate between the right and wrong paths and actions for you in your life.

Your Universal Day Number

Every day of your life holds a potential that is ripe for that moment in time. How to recognize this potential, appreciate it and then capture and learn from it are all a part of the essential aims of the numerological quest. Discovering your universal day number is also a part of this quest.

To arrive at your universal day number, you simply add your universal month number to your calendar day number.

Universal Month + Calendar Day = Universal Day

Therefore, if the date is **5th April 1993**, and your universal month number is, for the sake of example, two, then, you simply add 2 + 5 (5th April) to arrive at **7**. Seven is the universal day number in this instance. Once again, it would be wise to contemplate the meaning of seven before the day begins, and then to synchronize and attune yourself to the potential around you that this number represents.

Your Personal Day Number

Your personal day number holds a special meaning and significance to you and you alone. This number is another that, in the ancient numerology schools, was sometimes kept a closely guarded secret, divulged only after a hard-earned initiation. Every day has a personal meaning to you, and in ancient times, to be given a clue as to the meaning of each day you may have had to prove you were ready for such an honour.

To arrive at the personal day number, you add the current personal month number to the current calendar day number.

Personal Month	+	Calendar Day	=	Personal Day

For the purposes of illustration, let us assume that your personal month number is a six and that the date is **2nd April 1993**. Therefore, your personal day number would be 6 + 2 (personal month number + calendar day number), which equals **8**. Eight is the personal day number in this instance. You would therefore be most wise to turn within yourself and examine yourself according to the meaning of eight. What are your strengths and weaknesses, according to the power of eight? What do you neglect? Do you compensate well enough? Are you overcompensating? Questions such as these are the basis for a gentle self-analysis each day, directed according to the number of that day.

Essence Numbers

There is in numerology another equation for each daily cycle of life which identifies the *essential potential* and *essential lessons* of the day. This number is a personal number and therefore has a personal meaning and significance to you and you alone.

It is very easy when studying numerology to become overwhelmed by the amount of numbers in your life. If this is how you feel, you may wish to select just a few numbers to concentrate on. A good selection would be your personal birthdate number, your universal and personal year numbers, and the *essence number* for each day. This would be a well-balanced approach to numerology.

To arrive at your personal essence number for each day in your life, you add your current personal year number to your current personal month number to your current personal day number.

Personal Year $+$ Personal Month $+$ Personal Day $=$ Essence Number

Once you know your personal essence number for a day, it is possible then to perform a rewarding and enriching three-stage daily numerology exercise.

The first stage is performed at dawn, or at the beginning of your day. At this time you take time and make space to contemplate the meanings and significance of your personal essence number for the day to come. This is a wonderful way of preparing for the fullness of the day to come. You are training your perception to watch out for and recognize potential and opportunity. This is essential, because if you do not perceive something, it is for all intents and purposes not there.

The second stage is to use your personal essence number as a lens to focus on, perceive, watch and experience the world, both within and without, throughout the day. Whether you are at work, at home with the family, doing the house chores, or on holiday, you can use your essence number to inspire the way in which you relate to and experience the day that is today.

The third and final stage is at the end of the day, when you return to your essence number to review, reflect and think over the events of that day. What were the lessons

for you on this day? What did you do right? What did you
do wrong? What could you change? What could you keep?
These are the sorts of questions that are the most challenging of all; they are also the questions that provoke the most
rewarding answers.

Affinity Days

Within each and every given monthly cycle you have
affinity days. These affinity days are arrived at using a
slightly different method of calculation than that used to
determine the universal month and day, personal month
and day, and personal essence numbers. Affinity days
happen when your personal birthdate number is the same
as the number of the current calendar day.

During these moments of affinity, the potentials, possibilities and probabilities symbolized by your personal
birthdate number are more accessible, riper and more
pregnant that at other times. This is, in other words, a
good time for realizing and manifesting the power that is
symbolized by your personal birthdate number. On these
days you may experience your own *Eureka!* and your own
raison d'être.

One

If your personal birthdate number is a one, or if the
number one is prolific in your personal chart, then you
have affinity days on the 1st, 10th, 11th, 19th and 28th day
of each monthly cycle. On these days the potentials,
possibilities and probabilities associated with the number
one, such as creativity, originality, new beginnings and
new ventures, may all be especially evident. This may also
be a time for new ideas, plans and goals, and also for
re-dedication and recommitment. Direction, course and a

sure footing are especially important at this time, as progress, success and recognition are all due. If you are significantly influenced by the number one, it is especially important that you know who and what is *number one* in your life. These affinity days may give you clues.

Two

If your personal birthdate number is a two, or if the number two proliferates in your personal chart, then you have affinity days on the 2nd, 11th, 20th, 22nd and 29th day of each monthly cycle. On these days the meanings and significance of the number two, such as have to do with intuition, feeling, emotion and romance, may all be more obvious and more significant to you. These days of affinity may also be a time for listening to your innate, unconscious promptings and instincts. The time of two is also a time of the soul. Relationships of every kind can take a significant turn for the worse or for the better during the time of two. Two, being the power of duality, may mean you experience heightened joy or sadness on these days. Remember always, *you can decide*.

Three

If your personal birthdate number is a three, or if the number three appears many times in your personal chart, then you have affinity days on the 3rd, 12th, 21st and 30th day of each monthly cycle. On these days you may well make the power of three come alive in your life. Your active, progressive, outgoing and naturally optimistic qualities may thrive. Your keen mind, ever logical, rational and intellectual, may serve you well. The success and 'natural' (more like hard-earned) good fortune associated with the number three may also surface. You will always be successful, but at what? Some types of success are fulfilling; others are not. Have you the mental wisdom and cunning to discriminate between the two?

Four

If your personal birthdate number is a four, or if the number four has a strong presence in your personal chart, then you have affinity days on the 4th, 13th, 22nd and 31st day of each monthly cycle. On these days the strength of four is most likely to be the order of the day. Work, action, endeavour, will, attention to detail and consistent and persistent commitment will bring deserved results. Your enthusiasm, energy and natural sparkle and magnetism may well also thrive. You may ask yourself on these days, What is it that I really would like to work towards in my life? What are the causes in my life? To what shall I really dedicate my life?

Five

If your personal birthdate number is a five, or if the number five is abundant in your personal chart, then you have affinity days on the 5th, 14th and 23rd day of each monthly cycle. On these days you may well experience an affinity with communication, travel, journeys, meetings, groups, organizations and teams. As a number five person, you already have the potential to be very versatile and successful at most things you turn your hand to. On these affinity days you may find your natural versatility peaks all the more. Your links to the collective, to humanity, and also to selfless service and the support of others may again start you thinking on these days about what it is you really would like to aim for in life. Your ability to channel communication, inspiration, creativity and healing, in the broadest sense, may also transpire.

Six

If your personal birthdate number is a six, or if the number six appears many times in your personal chart, then you have affinity days on the 6th, 15th and 24th day of each monthly cycle. On these days try to be wise; look for the wisdom in all that exists in your life; and let wisdom be your guiding star. What are the ideals that move and motivate you? Are these ideals your own? Can they be attained? What direction must you take? What are the obstacles, both around you and within you? Your potential revolves around inspiration, excellence, innovation and insight. To the person who is significantly influenced by the number six, life is like a game of chess, so use these days to make your master moves.

Seven

If your personal birthdate number is a seven, or if the number seven is significantly present in your personal chart, then you have affinity days on the 7th, 16th and 25th day of each monthly cycle. These days may inspire the philosopher and poet in you. You may easily perform your best work on these days; and you may find you invoke a deeply subconscious power within you, experiencing a seventh heaven, perhaps. Keynotes for these days will be romance, love and fusion. These affinity days may well be a good time to be still, to contemplate, take time alone, relax inwardly and meditate a while on life. As well as working on your relationship with yourself, this may also be a good time to work consciously on your relationships with others. Realization, unfolding, discovery and profundity are also themes for these days.

Eight

If your personal birthdate number is an eight, or if the number eight can be counted many times in your personal chart, then you have affinity days on the 8th, 17th and 26th day of each monthly cycle. On these days of affinity you may do well to analyse your ability to manage, organize and network. How well do you hold your life together? Is there a pattern you have carved out for yourself? If not, why not? How can you begin? These questions are important to you. Direction is vitally important, and being able to integrate this direction with the world around you is also important. Paying attention to the spiritual is also a major theme for those of us who are significantly influenced by the number eight. On these days it is good to view the world from a spiritual viewpoint. What are the spiritual lessons in life right now?

Nine

If your personal birthdate number is a nine, or if the number nine has a significant appearance in your personal chart, then you have affinity days on the 9th, 18th and 27th day of each monthly cycle. Your perception, the watching mechanism within you, your ability to discriminate, the power to make appropriate decisions and the chance to examine and assess are all potentials of the number nine which might be alive on these special affinity days. Attention to detail, realism and practicality could be keynotes for these days. Summary, conclusions and endings, reviews, revisions and reflections: these are the flavours of the number nine potential. Imagine, if you will, a *Higher Self*, or a higher you, that can help you see the wood for the trees. These days can also be a time for setting sail towards new resolutions and horizons. However, before you plan your next port of call, take time to rest a while, assimilate previous experiences, and then, with reflection at the stern and forethought at the helm, you will be better prepared for your journey.

APPENDIX A

SAMPLE NUMEROLOGY CHARTS

Now let us take a look at the numerology charts of fourteen renowned people. Putting into practice that which the earlier chapters of this book has explained in theory will show you the power of numerology and the way in which a study of one's numerological chart can promote self-understanding. At the end of this section you will find a blank personal numerology chart, on which you can fill in details of your personal birthdate and name numbers. Appendix B offers a quick-reference guide to the significance of your numbers; Appendix C is an index of the number profiles of many prominent celebrities of the past and present.

Ronald Reagan

Ronald Wilson Reagan was President of the United States of America from 1981 to 1989. During his time in office there were many rumours that both he and his wife, Nancy Reagan, turned to astrologers for advice from the stars. No such rumours were ever spread concerning numerologists and the potential influence of numbers on the Reagans' lives. This is a great pity, because their numerology charts make fascinating reading.

NAME: _____

_____

_____

_____

_____

PERSONAL NAME NUMBER: _____

DATE OF BIRTH: _____

_____

_____

_____

_____

PERSONAL BIRTHDATE NUMBER: _____

HIGHER LAW _____

SPIRITUAL _____ PHYSICAL _____

LOVE _____ EMOTIONAL _____

WISDOM _____ MENTAL _____

COLLECTIVE _____ WILL _____

Ronald Reagan was born on the 6th February 1911. His personal birthdate number is the number two. The number two is a symbol for the potential of emotions, feeling and soul. It is a feminine potential which works with instincts, intuitions and hunches. It is also a creative potential. Ronald Reagan has two number twos in his chart. Two number twos are often a clue that decision-making and problem-solving are highly influenced by either emotion, feeling, intuition and/or soul. In other words, Ronald Reagan may use his feelings more than his intellect to make decisions.

As described in Chapter 5, numerology holds that there are three major life stages, each lasting for approximately twenty-seven years. The *birth day number* represents a potential for the first stage of life; the *birth month number* represents a potential for the second stage of life; and the *birth year number* represents a potential for the third stage of life. It is interesting to note that Ronald Reagan's second stage of life is also ruled by the number two. Furthermore, Ronald Reagan's personal name number is also a number two.

Ronald Reagan's interest in politics became public during his second stage of life. He was made governor of California in 1966, defeating Edmund G. Brown, who himself had previously beaten Richard Nixon for the same office. Reagan did this at a time when his second stage of life was about to end. This was possibly excellent timing for him, as his third stage of life is ruled by the number three, an excellent potential for success, social appearance, mental dexterity and also mercurial wit. Ronald Reagan was to call upon all of these potentials during his pursuit of the presidency.

Although the number two is the ruling number of Ronald Reagan's chart, there is no doubting that, considering the six appearances of the number one, number one is the *ruling influence*. The number one potential often promotes ambition and a desire to be successful. It also inspires the leader and patriot in a person. Ronald Reagan was first successful as a radio sports announcer, then as a film actor, and then as a politician. His leadership qualities abounded. His desire for America to be number one in the world was also obvious.

Ronald Reagan has no number of will (four). The fact that he had six number ones certainly would make up for this deficit. Also, the chart of his second wife, Nancy Reagan, includes two number fours. The belief that Nancy was the power behind the presidency has some support here. Another 'partner' of Ronald Reagan's, Margaret Thatcher, actually has three number fours in her chart. This sheds some light on their relationship and mutual attraction.

Ronald Reagan has no power of seven in his chart; Nancy Reagan has one power of seven. Once again, they seem to complement each other well. Neither has a power of five, however. This number may be filled by family members, thus adding to their harmony. Or perhaps they are both attracted to number five friends. This is a definite possibility, as we are all attracted to one degree or another by our opposites. Opposites attract because they often can make peace for one another.

Margaret Thatcher

Margaret Thatcher became Britain's first woman Prime Minister following the general election of May 1979. She remained in office for eleven years, during which time she pioneered a new political and economic philosophy, termed 'Thatcherism'. Her relentless endeavour and firm method of rule earned her the nickname 'the iron lady'. It

NAME: _____

_____

_____

_____

_____

PERSONAL NAME NUMBER: _____

DATE OF BIRTH: _____

_____

_____

_____

_____

PERSONAL BIRTHDATE NUMBER: _____

HIGHER LAW _____

SPIRITUAL _____ PHYSICAL _____

LOVE _____ EMOTIONAL _____

WISDOM _____ MENTAL _____

COLLECTIVE _____ WILL _____

is perhaps not too surprising, then, to discover that Margaret Thatcher's personal birthdate number is the number four.

The number four potential often inspires unswerving application, complete commitment and dogged determination. The rumour that during her time in office Margaret Thatcher only slept four hours a night seems apt! It is also interesting to note that Margaret Thatcher's personal name number is also a four. Furthermore, the power of four appears three times in her chart. This would imply a potential for mental strength, will and toughness. It would be fair to say that Margaret Thatcher was both loved and loathed for these qualities.

As for Ronald Reagan, Margaret Thatcher's *ruling influence* in her numerology chart is the number one, which appears six times. The number one inspires leadership and a desire for success. First as a chemist, then in law, and then in politics, Margaret Thatcher has enjoyed her share of success. It is interesting to note that the number one appears in all three stages of her life: in the thirteen, the ten and the 1925. It would seem that this power and potential will be active for all of her life.

When you combine the three fours with the six ones, you have an awesome potential for will, endeavour and sheer brute strength. The potential here is both powerful and mighty. It is also interesting to note that Margaret Thatcher has twelve masculine numbers as opposed to five feminine numbers in her chart. The masculine portrayal of Margaret Thatcher as seen in the satire series *Spitting Image*, dressed in a suit and smoking a cigar, enjoyed mass appeal because it touched a truth.

In numerology there is the kingdom of Light and the kingdom of Shadows. In Margaret Thatcher's shadow chart, the six number ones turn to six number eights. Eight symbolizes a potential for management, organization, control and authority. The number eight is also the *ruling influence* of Margaret Thatcher's third stage of life which began 1979 or thereabouts, the year she was first elected Prime Minister. This power of eight also holds a spiritual potential. This can manifest only if the six number ones and the three number fours are properly controlled.

Margaret Thatcher has no number six in her numerology chart. This is partly compensated for by the fact that the number one appears six times, and is thus ruled by the six. Also, Margaret Thatcher's husband Denis has two number sixes in his numerology chart. Denis Thatcher has no number eight, whereas Margaret Thatcher has one number eight. It would appear, therefore, that they share a potential to be able to support and complement one another well.

It is perhaps surprising to note that Denis Thatcher, like his wife, also has six number ones.

Prince Charles

Prince Charles, His Royal Highness the Prince of Wales, is the eldest son of Queen Elizabeth II, and is, thereby, heir-apparent to the throne of the United Kingdom. Prince Charles' personal birthdate number is the number two, a symbol for emotion, feeling, intuition, soul and feminine potentials.

The number two often promotes a desire for things that are alternative and/or complementary. Prince Charles' interest in alternative and complementary medicines, in environmental debates and campaigns, and in orthodox and unorthodox spiritual teachings, is evidence which supports this potential influence of number two. The ability to be both open- and broad-minded are also potentials that are promoted by the number two.

The number two has a soul potential. Prince Charles has

NAME: _____

_____

_____

_____

_____

PERSONAL NAME NUMBER: _____

DATE OF BIRTH: _____

_____

_____

_____

_____

PERSONAL BIRTHDATE NUMBER: _____

HIGHER LAW _____

SPIRITUAL _____   PHYSICAL _____

LOVE _____   EMOTIONAL _____

WISDOM _____   MENTAL _____

COLLECTIVE _____   WILL _____

been described as 'a modern man in search of a soul'. His campaign to put the soul back into modern architecture, his interests in the ethics, morals and standards of education, his respect for the arts, and also his association with such people as Sir Laurens van der Post, explorer, philosopher and author of *Venture to the Interior* and many other books, may all have been influenced and supported by the number two potential.

There are four number twos in Prince Charles' numerology chart. This means that the number two is governed by the power of four. In other words, the feeling and soul potential is governed by the power of will, determination and endeavour. It is highly likely, therefore, that Prince Charles will be motivated by the number two in almost everything he undertakes. This theory is enhanced by the fact that the number four appears twice in his chart, and is therefore governed by the power of two.

The *ruling influence* in Prince Charles' numerology chart is neither the number two or the number four, but rather the number one, which appears six times. It is highly appropriate for an explorer, adventurer, keen sportsman, national figurehead and possible future monarch to have the backing of so many number ones. These six number ones turn to six number eights in Prince Charles' shadow chart, which points to possible inner, innate potentials. It is highly likely that the eight potential will be activated as life progresses, mainly because of the presence of four soulful number twos in the chart. Four twos add up to eight, which also enhances this possible relationship and potential.

NAME: _____

_____

_____

_____

_____

PERSONAL NAME NUMBER: _____

DATE OF BIRTH: _____

_____

_____

_____

_____

PERSONAL BIRTHDATE NUMBER: _____

HIGHER LAW _____

SPIRITUAL _____   PHYSICAL _____

LOVE _____   EMOTIONAL _____

WISDOM _____   MENTAL _____

COLLECTIVE _____   WILL _____

Princess Diana

Prince Charles and the then Diana Spencer were married in 1981. Their romance was likened at the time to a fairy tale and Arthurian legend. And almost everyone was invited to the wedding, courtesy of television.

Prince Charles and Princess Diana share the two most romantic potentials as their personal birthdate number. Prince Charles has the number two, Princess Diana the number seven. The relationship between the number two and the number seven contains within it the drama of love. Number two symbolizes a potential for soulful love, but also the potential for emotional, turbulent love. The number seven symbolizes a potential for spiritual, unconditional love, but also, once again, a potential for emotional, turbulent love.

Because Prince Charles is a number two and Princess Diana a number seven, they have a very powerful potential to support and harmonize, or to disagree and divide. As individuals, both Prince Charles and Princess Diana will have to control the relationship between two and seven. For Prince Charles the number two appears four times in his chart, and thus the number seven will appear four times in his shadow chart. For Princess Diana the number seven appears three times in her chart, and thus the number two will appear three times in her shadow chart. Each will, therefore, experience the dramas of two and of seven, both in their individual lives and in their life together.

The attraction that one person feels for another can very often be deciphered and understood by numbers. It can be very beneficial, therefore, to compare charts with those of your loved ones. Princess Diana may well have been

NAME: _____

_____

_____

_____

_____

PERSONAL NAME NUMBER: _____

DATE OF BIRTH: _____

_____

_____

_____

_____

PERSONAL BIRTHDATE NUMBER: _____

HIGHER LAW _____

SPIRITUAL _____   PHYSICAL _____

LOVE _____   EMOTIONAL _____

WISDOM _____   MENTAL _____

COLLECTIVE _____   WILL _____

attracted to Prince Charles because his chart compensates for and balances hers in a number of ways. Diana has no number twos; Charles has four. Diana has no number fours; Charles has two. And Diana has no number five; while Charles has one. Thus, Prince Charles certainly has a potential to provide for and support his Princess.

Conversely, Charles has no number six; Diana has two. Charles has only one number seven; Diana has three. And Charles has only one number eight; while Diana has two. Thus, Princess Diana has also the potential to strengthen, consolidate and compensate for the potentials and gaps in Prince Charles' numerology chart.

Neither Prince Charles nor Princess Diana has a number three. Thus, there is a potential for mental distance, disagreement and unrest between them. This does not have to be the case, but the fact that there is a potential for this is undeniable. Princess Diana's five number ones and Prince Charles' six number ones may also be potentials that either integrate or clash with one another. Much depends, once again, on the relationship between two and seven.

Marilyn Monroe

The life of Marilyn Monroe was at once very public and very private. Her every movement and action appeared to be so well detailed and well documented, yet there remains so much that was not divulged, that was discreet and may forever remain undiscovered. The lady who was born Norma Jean Martenson and who later became Marilyn Monroe lived a life that was both social and solitary, glamorous and tragic.

Marilyn Monroe's personal birthdate number is the number seven, which is a symbol for the potential of love,

NAME: _____

_____

_____

_____

_____

PERSONAL NAME NUMBER: _____

DATE OF BIRTH: _____

_____

_____

_____

_____

PERSONAL BIRTHDATE NUMBER: _____

HIGHER LAW _____

SPIRITUAL _____   PHYSICAL _____

LOVE _____   EMOTIONAL _____

WISDOM _____   MENTAL _____

COLLECTIVE _____   WILL _____

the spirit of romance, poetic philosophy and spiritual depth. Marilyn Monroe's enormous popularity and success in films such as *The Seven Year Itch* were perfect vehicles for this potential. She was described by some, unjustly perhaps, as a 'sex goddess'. There are plenty of people who would, on the other hand, describe her talent as the ability to convey the essence of romantic, poetic and spiritual love.

The number seven appears two times in Marilyn Monroe's numerology chart, and therefore the seven is governed by the two. Here, once again, there is evidence of the grand drama of love as enacted by the numbers two and seven. The conflict between spiritual, soulful love and physical, emotional love is the potential conflict of these two numbers. Did Marilyn Monroe portray spiritual love? Or was it mere sex appeal? Were people attracted to the sevens of Marilyn Monroe or to the twos? The debate has still not lost its momentum.

The number seven can promote the loner in you, for good or bad reasons. Marilyn Monroe lived her early life in a string of orphanages, very much alone. Her successes, as actress and star, great as they were, still left her feeling alone. As for her death, well, she probably did die lonely, but the real truth about her death may never be known. Marilyn Monroe was a loner. Her third husband, the American playwright Arthur Miller, wrote *The Misfits* especially for her. In this film Marilyn portrayed a girl who felt innately remote, distant, and lonely—ultimately, a misfit.

Marilyn Monroe's numerology chart is interesting because of what is *not* there. There is no three, four or five. No number three certainly would not have done much to save her from her so-called 'dumb blonde' reputation. No number four may well have been compensated for by the four number ones in her chart. Having no number five, i.e. no humanity or collective potential, may well be the reason why she felt such a loner.

Arthur Miller

Arthur Miller is one of the most powerful and evocative playwrights of modern times. His works include *Death of a Salesman*, which won the 1949 Pulitzer Prize, *The Crucible*, an indictment of McCarthyism, and *After the Fall*, which is in part autobiographical of his life with Marilyn Monroe.

Arthur Miller's personal birthdate number is the number seven. His personal name number is the number two. Once again, then, we have the seven and two revolving one around the other. There is great potential for both these potentials to work in harmony and in unison with one another. So often, though, this potential is only ever occasionally realized. That this relationship between two and seven is a potential source of inspiration for his writing is certainly not out of the question.

Arthur Miller has three number sevens in his numerology chart. The seven potential is therefore quite prominent. Three sevens also means that Arthur Miller has a potential to use mental, rational control to protect the seven potential. The challenge is to ensure that the three does not eclipse, overshadow and thereby submerge the seven potential.

The *ruling influence* in Arthur Miller's numerology chart is the number one, which appears a total of seven times and is thus governed by the number seven. Seven number ones may either serve to earth the power of spiritual love or sink it. As always, the potential is there for all types of growth. Experience will have a profound affect on whether, when and how this potential will develop.

NAME: _____

_____

_____

_____

_____

PERSONAL NAME NUMBER: _____

DATE OF BIRTH: _____

_____

_____

_____

_____

PERSONAL BIRTHDATE NUMBER: _____

HIGHER LAW _____

SPIRITUAL _____   PHYSICAL _____

LOVE _____   EMOTIONAL _____

WISDOM _____   MENTAL _____

COLLECTIVE _____   WILL _____

Like Arthur Miller, Marilyn Monroe's personal birth-date number is also the number seven. This they share in common. It may have been their mutual attraction. The two nines, two sixes and one eight they also have in common might have drawn them together. Arthur Miller has no number two; Marilyn Monroe compensated with one number two. Marilyn Monroe had no number five; Arthur Miller compensated with one number five.

Marilyn Monroe may have seen in Arthur Miller the cultured, spiritual and poetic dimensions of her own nature. She appeared so frivolous and yet so fearfully profound. Neither Arthur Miller nor Marilyn Monroe had numbers three or four. It may therefore have been difficult for them to enjoy both mental agreement and an agreement of will and direction in life. Their relationship appears to have been both complementary and contrasting. These numbers suggest that paradox was a particular feature of Marilyn Monroe's whole life.

Sigmund Freud

The nineteenth-century neurologist Sigmund Freud revolutionized the way we look at ourselves. Through his pioneering efforts he founded psychoanalysis, promoting a number of theories and hypotheses which have changed the course of modern psychology. Thanks to Freud, our knowledge and understanding of ourselves has been challenged, transformed and changed. Whether you like or dislike the man, agree or disagree with his theories, support or dispute his method of research and experimentation, the fact remains that Freud transfigured our way of interpreting ourselves.

Sigmund Freud's personal birthdate number is the number four, a symbol for the potential of will, determination,

NAME: _____

_____

_____

_____

_____

PERSONAL NAME NUMBER: _____

DATE OF BIRTH: _____

_____

_____

_____

_____

PERSONAL BIRTHDATE NUMBER: _____

HIGHER LAW _____

SPIRITUAL _____   PHYSICAL _____

LOVE _____   EMOTIONAL _____

WISDOM _____   MENTAL _____

COLLECTIVE _____   WILL _____

persistence and commitment. Sigmund Freud had to draw upon all of his reserves of strength and application to fight off the conservative opposition of the day to his new ideas and theories. Much of his work was totally new to the Western world. He has been described as 'the Copernicus of the Mind'. For many years Freud had to work alone and in isolation because of his beliefs.

The *ruling influence* in Sigmund Freud's numerology chart is shared between three number ones and three number twos. It is wholly fitting that these two numbers should share the ruling influence of his chart. The number one is very much a physical potential. It represents, among other things, ego, ambition and drive. Sigmund Freud coined the terms *id*, *ego* and *superego* to describe a fundamental makeup of the human personality. Briefly put, the id represents the innocent, instinctive and sensual child within you. The ego represents the socially conscious adult within you. And the superego, or ego-ideal, represents the conscience, *Higher Self* or parent within you. Sigmund Freud believed that one common cause of neurosis was the failure of the ego to mediate between the id and the superego.

Sigmund Freud's psychology was also a psychology of drives. He coined the word *libido* to help to describe his belief that a person is driven by innate, instinctive drives that are mainly related to sex and aggression. The number one potential can promote sexual attraction and pursuit, and also physical strength and aggression. Sigmund Freud's psychology has been criticized by some as a 'physical psychology' that caters well for the physical, emotional and mental but which overlooks the spiritual almost completely.

The number two is the other ruling influence in Sigmund Freud's numerology chart. This too is very interesting, because the number two is a potential for, among other things, the unconscious. Sigmund Freud 'discovered' the unconscious mind. It was Sigmund Freud who first posited the theory that it is within the realms of the unconscious that many neuroses and conflicts first begin to develop. Sigmund Freud explored hypnosis and then later worked with free association and dreams, which he described as 'The royal road to the unconscious', in an attempt to explore and heal the unconscious minds of his patients.

Another important influence in Sigmund Freud's numerology chart is the number six, which appears twice. The number six is also Sigmund Freud's personal name number. It is perhaps not fashionable today to describe Sigmund Freud as a wise man. If, however, one remembers that his work was that of a pioneer, that he was a revolutionary, and that much of his work has become the basis and the catalyst for almost every other school of modern psychology, then perhaps it is fair to describe Sigmund Freud as a wise man for his time.

Sigmund Freud has no power of seven in his numerology chart. This is also interesting to note, because Sigmund Freud's psychology had little or nothing to do with concepts of love. His view of humanity was essentially pessimistic. And yet, in the seventh major cycle of his life, when the number seven would have potentially been active, Sigmund Freud began to change his ideas a little. It was Freud who said late in his life, 'In the final analysis, in order not to fall ill we must learn to love.'

Carl Jung

Carl Jung was more than a psychologist. His life was a quest for evidence and for ways to achieve unity, cohesion, wholeness and belonging in the world. His quest

NAME: _____
_____
_____
_____
_____

PERSONAL NAME NUMBER: _____

DATE OF BIRTH: _____
_____
_____
_____

PERSONAL BIRTHDATE NUMBER: _____

HIGHER LAW _____

SPIRITUAL _____ PHYSICAL _____

LOVE _____ EMOTIONAL _____

WISDOM _____ MENTAL _____

COLLECTIVE _____ WILL _____

took him to the regions of philosophy, metaphysics, arch-aeology, theology, symbolism, the occult, alchemy, music, art, and beyond. Carl Jung's life has often been compared to and contrasted with the life of his one-time mentor, Sigmund Freud. Both their numerology charts highlight interesting similarities and also distinct differences.

Carl Jung's personal birthdate number is the number nine, which is a symbol for truth and spiritual truth, law and spiritual law, research and discrimination. Carl Jung dedicated his life to the search for human truths and human laws. The number nine is also a symbol for the *Higher Self*. Carl Jung's psychology was in part a psychology of the Higher Self. His concepts of teleology and individuation described a belief that the human self is inevitably bound on a journey towards wholeness, realization and the achievement and awareness of a Higher Self.

The *ruling influence* of Carl Jung's numerology chart is the number one, a symbol for the pioneer and explorer. Carl Jung was a great explorer, both of the worlds around him and the worlds within him. The number one in his chart appears three times, and is thus governed by the power of three, which means that his physical energy, ambitions and determination would probably have been highly influenced by mental considerations. The mind was Jung's territory and terrain. The number one was a shared ruling influence in Sigmund Freud's numerology chart.

The number five appears twice in Carl Jung's numerology chart and is also his personal name number. The number five stands for the collective, the group and humanity. Carl Jung agreed with Sigmund Freud's map of the mind, at first. He later saw fit to divide the unconscious mind into a *personal unconscious* and a *collective unconscious*. Carl Jung's theories of the collective unconscious and of collective archetypes are his most famous. It is wholly fitting that the 'psychologist of collectives' should have such a strong collective influence in his numerology chart.

You cannot help but notice when you look at Carl Jung's numerology chart how well developed the higher numbers are. There are, in total, three fives, two sixes, two sevens, two eights and two nines. Thus the spiritual side of Carl Jung's chart suggests a very powerful potential. It is also well earthed by the three ones, the two twos and the one three. Carl Jung's view of humanity was essentially very positive and hopeful, much more so than that of Sigmund Freud. The numbers of their charts suggest a potential for this to be so.

Carl Jung had no number four, symbol of personal will, in his numerology chart. However, the appearance of three number fives, symbol of collective will, suggests a potential to put collective will before individual will. This too is an accurate observation of Carl Jung's life, which he dedicated wholly and selflessly to his vision and belief of a collective, single humanity and a collective, single world.

Ernest Hemingway

Ernest Hemingway holds a place in modern history as the most inspiring, intriguing and influential American writer of his generation. Born on 21st July 1899 in Illinois, Ernest Hemingway's personal birthdate number is the number one. The ruling number of his numerology chart is also the number one, which appears six times. The essential potentials of number one were evident everywhere throughout Ernest Hemingway's experience of life.

Although he married several times, and although he had many famous 'friendships', notably with Scott Fitzgerald, Ezra Pound, Gertrude Stein and other American expatriates living in Paris, Ernest Hemingway lived the life of a

NAME: _____

_____

_____

_____

_____

PERSONAL NAME NUMBER: _____

DATE OF BIRTH: _____

_____

_____

_____

_____

PERSONAL BIRTHDATE NUMBER: _____

HIGHER LAW _____

SPIRITUAL _____   PHYSICAL _____

LOVE _____   EMOTIONAL _____

WISDOM _____   MENTAL _____

COLLECTIVE _____   WILL _____

loner. He was a 'one-off', belligerent and bullying, honest and helpful, satirical and sincere, scathing and supportive. Much of his work was inspired by loneliness and isolation, which he described as occupational hazards of writing; much of his life was afflicted by depression and despair, and ended ultimately in suicide.

Ernest Hemingway was a creative cavalier and intrepid explorer, whose greatest work of drama was his own well-documented life. True to the potential of number one, Ernest Hemingway lived life to the limit. The bull fighting of *Death in the Afternoon*; the big-game hunting in *The Green Hills of Africa*; the high seas of *The Old Man and the Sea*; the Spanish wartime adventures of *For Whom the Bell Tolls*, spy networks in Cuba and FBI files; romance, adultery, impotence, venereal disease and homo-sexuality—Ernest Hemingway either experienced it all or saw it all, and he definitely wrote it all.

Ernest Hemingway's style of writing and living were remarkably similar. Fact, fiction and fantasy often flowed into one. His short stories, in particular, were written in a naked, abrupt, harsh and unsentimental style. Ernest Hemingway always advised his audience to read his books twice—once to take in the words that were written, and once to take in the words that were not. He often maintained that what was left out was more important than what was left in.

When examining Ernest Hemingway's numerology chart it is interesting to note there are two zeros and no four, five or six. So many gaps may also have lent to the loneliness and isolation that Ernest Hemingway never learned to live with. Whenever there are no number fives in a numerology chart there is, in particular, a potential for an innate sense of loneliness, of not belonging.

Three number nines is a powerful symbol for the archetypes of judge and judgement. Ernest Hemingway measured, judged and evaluated everybody and everything. No part of life was left unexperienced or unexamined. He was renowned for direct, honest, open opinion. He never hesitated to take sides. He was, in particular, his own most severe critic.

Three nines is a powerful, pure potential that can often inspire a sense of mission and an experience of spiritual, Higher Self. Hemingway wrestled with these potentials throughout all of his life and work. Another common potential of the number nine, especially three nines, is a tendency to live as a law unto oneself. Ernest Hemingway, the 'one-man show', was ungraceful but genuine, sworn to his own truth, and ultimately, very definitely, a living law unto himself.

The Nobel Prize for Literature in 1954, and the Pulitzer Prize in 1952 for *The Old Man and the Sea*, were just rewards for a man who was both possessed and inspired by a ruthless, uncompromising spirit of creative enterprise and dangerous adventure. Ernest Hemingway's numbers help to cast light upon the life of a man who was universally appreciated but seldom understood.

Vincent van Gogh

The Dutch painter Vincent van Gogh was born on 30th March 1853. He, like Ernest Hemingway, was an artist who sacrificed life for art. His pictures of blazing, pure colour and simple, non-dimensional form were a therapy, a release and an expression for an inner turbulent tide and trauma. Here, on canvas, the world became witness to a man's private pursuit of purging himself of his woe.

Vincent an Gogh's personal birthdate number is the number five, which also appears twice in his numerology chart. The five potential often inspires the inner archetypes

NAME: _____

_____

_____

_____

PERSONAL NAME NUMBER: _____

DATE OF BIRTH: _____

_____

_____

_____

PERSONAL BIRTHDATE NUMBER: _____

HIGHER LAW _____

SPIRITUAL _____ PHYSICAL _____

LOVE _____ EMOTIONAL _____

WISDOM _____ MENTAL _____

COLLECTIVE _____ WILL _____

of communicator and artist. Art for art's sake is usually not enough for a number five person; the art of a number five person often sets out to shock, surprise and confront. It is an art that conveys truths, communicates ideas, shares visions and inspires lessons. Vincent van Gogh's art achieved all of these things.

The *ruling influence* of Vincent van Gogh's numerology chart is the number three, which symbolizes a potential that includes mind, thought, logic, ideas and mental creativity. Because the number three appears four times in Vincent van Gogh's chart, the three potential is strongly influenced by a potential of will, effort and endeavour. This rare arrangement of numbers makes for a very powerful potential that might easily topple a person. Without proper control such a strong potential in a person could burn so bright as to blow.

When looking at a numerology chart it is always interesting to assess the relationship, order and balance between the number two of emotions and the number three of mind. Vincent van Gogh has four threes but no twos. Such a prominent mental power of three would definitely be potentially problematic without any emotional support. The physical number one is also powered by the number three because it appears three times, thus serving to further accentuate the imbalance between three and two.

The number thirty may have been a particularly active potential during Vincent van Gogh's first stage of life, which lasts for the first 27 years of life. Thirty is made up of a three and a zero, the combination of which can symbolize unique mental originality, primordial mental instinct and creative mental power. The second stage of life is also symbolized by the potential of three (March). And it is also interesting to note that Vincent van Gogh committed suicide aged thirty-seven, in the first year after his third major life cycle, the cycle of mind.

Vincent van Gogh has two eights in his numerology

chart, and his personal name number is also eight. He therefore has three eights overall, which suggests a close connection between the spiritual (eight) and the mental (three). Vincent van Gogh, the son of a Calvinist preacher, was employed as an evangelist on the Belgian coalfields before turning to art. Through his letters to his brother Theo readers are struck by the spiritual suffering of an artist too sensitive and fragile to survive this world.

Elizabeth Taylor

Elizabeth Taylor, the child movie star who became a mature dramatic actress, has lived a public life all of her life. Her films, which include *National Velvet* (1944), *Cleopatra* (1962) and *Who's Afraid of Virginia Woolf?* (1966), the latter two made with Richard Burton, achieved popular success and critical acclaim. However, of all the dramas Elizabeth Taylor has played, her audiences will agree that nothing has been quite as tempestuous, tragic or theatrical as the drama of her own life.

Whenever a person's personal birthdate and name number are the same, the potential of that number tends to be prevalent and very powerful in his or her life. Elizabeth Taylor's personal birthdate and name number are both eight. The potential of the number eight holds a feminine, spiritual, creative and healing potential. This potential can often promote ethereal, spiritual and psychic sensitivity, particularly if the eight is not eclipsed by its shadow power of one.

Elizabeth Taylor has two *ruling influences* in her numerology chart, which are four ones and four twos. The number one is perhaps appropriate for a starlet of the cinema screen whose entire life has been captured by writers, directors, biographers, editors and cameramen. A

NAME: _____

_____

_____

_____

_____

PERSONAL NAME NUMBER: _____

DATE OF BIRTH: _____

_____

_____

_____

_____

PERSONAL BIRTHDATE NUMBER: _____

HIGHER LAW _____

SPIRITUAL _____ PHYSICAL _____

LOVE _____ EMOTIONAL _____

WISDOM _____ MENTAL _____

COLLECTIVE _____ WILL _____

number one that appears four times tends to be a very powerful potential for ambition, will, direction and endeavour. Four ones may help to balance and compensate for the absence of four in Elizabeth Taylor's chart.

Perhaps the most interesting feature of her numerology chart is the shared ruling influence of four twos. Two is the number of drama, play, theatre and the stage. Many of the greatest actors and actresses of the world have a prominent two potential in their numerology charts. This potential may help them, for instance, to act, empathize, feel, project, role play, work with, combine, understand, imitate and become.

Two is also the number of emotion and soul, union or conflict, bonding or division. Elizabeth Taylor has appeared emotionally sensitive and vulnerable throughout her life. Her marriages up until now have failed to provide her with the harmony, happiness and wholeness her heart has longed for.

The number two is also represented in Elizabeth Taylor's first two stages of life. The first stage, covering approximately the first twenty-seven years of life, is represented by the birthday number, which is twenty-seven. Twenty-seven is the classic symbol of the archetypal drama of emotional and spiritual love. The teaching of twenty-seven is that inner harmony is the basis for harmony with and between others. Two and seven can live peacefully only if emotion and feeling are prepared to listen to spirit and soul.

Elizabeth Taylor's second stage of life, from approximately twenty-seven to fifty-four, is represented by the birth month number, which is two. The third stage of life, from approximately fifty-four to eighty-one, is represented by the birth year number, which has a two in it but which adds up to six—the number of wisdom. The lifeline of six may well offer a potential for Elizabeth Taylor to learn, understand and accept the lessons of her life. Six is a time to be wise.

Richard Burton

The world-famous fiery Welsh actor whose turbulent on again/off again relationships with, among others, Elizabeth Taylor, and whose stage and screen performances are the stuff of theatrical history, was born on the 10th November 1925. His personal birthdate number is the number two, which is highly appropriate for a man whose dramatic acting talents led him to achieve notoriety and acclaim.

Richard Burton portrayed some of the most angry, hostile, embittered, tormented and emotion-driven characters found in history and fiction. His performances in films such as *Alexander the Great* (1956), *Look Back in Anger* (1959), *Cleopatra* (1962), *Becket* (1964) and *Equus* (1977), among many others, provided him with a means of exploring, empathizing with and projecting a whole gamut of human strengths and weaknesses. His sheer magnetism was mesmerizing.

Such presence, stature and charisma, as flowed so freely from this fine fellow, was doubtless fuelled by his *ruling influence* number, one. The power of one appears an astonishing eight times in Richard Burton's numerology chart. The potential of one, which includes ambition, originality, drive, direction, fire, energy and creativity, was obvious. And perhaps it was the eight ones that attracted Elizabeth Taylor, a number eight person, to Richard Burton. Having eight ones also points to a very powerful spiritual potential.

Throughout each of his three stages of life, Richard Burton's prevalent potential was the number one. In fact,

NAME: _____

_____

_____

_____

_____

PERSONAL NAME NUMBER: _____

DATE OF BIRTH: _____

_____

_____

_____

_____

PERSONAL BIRTHDATE NUMBER: _____

HIGHER LAW _____

SPIRITUAL _____   PHYSICAL _____

LOVE _____   EMOTIONAL _____

WISDOM _____   MENTAL _____

COLLECTIVE _____   WILL _____

when looking at his whole birthdate, four of the first five numbers are one, the other number being zero. Once again, this arrangement of numbers points to a tremendous possible aura of power, energy and magnetism. This potential of one is so strong that he may at times in his life have felt possessed and compelled by this inner, innate influence.

Richard Burton has three twos in his numerology chart, which once again emphasizes potentials of emotion, empathy, feeling and soul. His three twos would suggest a strong emotional drive that could potentially be protected and secured by a mental strength. With no number six, the three twos (3 x 2 = 6) might have meant Richard Burton was able to act wisely—whether he was really wise is another matter that only his closest colleagues, friends and loved ones would know.

The shape of Richard Burton's and Elizabeth Taylor's numerology charts is basically the same. The power of their personal charts is concentrated in the first two numbers. Such is the absolute nature of their arrangement of numbers that one and two might easily eclipse all other potentials. They share the same potentials for the numbers three, five, seven and eight, which suggests compatibility. However, neither has a four, and therefore personal will, endeavour, direction, building and support might not have met with harmony or agreement. For two such powerful personalities, an absence of four may well have been fatal.

Alfred Hitchcock

The British film director Sir Alfred Hitchcock was a master filmmaker whose camera and direction created, conjured up and conveyed unparalleled tension, fear and

NAME: _____

_____

_____

_____

_____

PERSONAL NAME NUMBER: _____

DATE OF BIRTH: _____

_____

_____

_____

_____

PERSONAL BIRTHDATE NUMBER: _____

HIGHER LAW ____

SPIRITUAL ____   PHYSICAL ____

LOVE ____   EMOTIONAL ____

WISDOM ____   MENTAL ____

COLLECTIVE ____   WILL ____

suspense. He specialized in the genres of sophisticated crime and psychological thriller, creating magnificent masterpieces such as *The Thirty-Nine Steps* (1935), *Notorious* (1946), *Strangers on a Train* (1951), *Dial M for Murder* (1953), *Rear Window* (1954), *Psycho* (1960) and *The Birds* (1963).

Hitchcock's personal birthdate number is the number three, the potential of which includes mental creativity, invention and ideas, concepts and imagination. The power of three is primarily a mental potential. Hitchcock was able to get into the minds of his writers, actors and audiences. His fast-moving, compelling creations were mental masterpieces filled with frames of trickery and deceit, insight and illusion, genius and insanity.

The number three appears three times in Hitchcock's numerology chart, thus representing a powerful mental potential. Three threes equals a nine. There are three nines in the full chart, and Hitchcock's personal name number is also a nine. Nine is a potential for the watching mechanism, for insight and pure perception. It can also be a potential for being a law unto oneself. Hitchcock will always be remembered as part English eccentric, part genius.

The *ruling influence* of Hitchcock's numerology chart is the number one, which appears four times. It would appear that Sir Alfred made good use of this potential to make films with a unique and inventive flair. Hitchcock's direction was an absolute inspiration to both audiences and fellow filmmakers. In particular, his work was of special interest to the creative and imaginative *New Wave* of French filmmakers of the 1950s.

The number two appears three times in Hitchcock's numerology chart. As with Elizabeth Taylor and Richard Burton, Sir Alfred may well have tapped into this potential of two to create drama, empathy, tension and conflict.

Three twos is often a numerological symbol for mental control over emotion. The master directors of film are able to control the emotions of their audiences through their mental devices. Hitchcock used a variety of techniques to achieve this aim, including subliminal scripts.

Most entertainers have a significant count of fives in their numerology chart, and many directors have a powerful presence of six. Hitchcock has neither. The lack of sixes could, however, be balanced by the threes, the shadow of which is six. The dearth of fives is not easily compensated by any other number in the chart. So often a person will unconsciously attempt to balance his or her numbers through relationships with people, places and work. Hitchcock played with potentials that gave cinema audiences unparalleled pleasure and alarm.

Steven Spielberg

Steven Spielberg was the most successful cinema screen director, both commercially and creatively, of the 1970s and 80s. He was born on 18th December 1947, which translates into a personal birthdate number of six. Six is a wisdom potential that is also commonly linked to the arts, editing, aesthetics, design, production and direction. That Spielberg should be born under the six potential is indeed apt.

The number one appears five times in Spielberg's numerology chart, and is therefore the *ruling influence*. The number one is a potential for invention, creativity and originality. It is also a potential for qualities of childlike innocence. This is interesting, because many of Spielberg's creations have captured a spirit of childhood innocence. *ET* (1982) and *Gremlins* (1984) are two modern childhood classics that appeal to all generations.

NAME: _____

_____

_____

_____

_____

PERSONAL NAME NUMBER: _____

DATE OF BIRTH: _____

_____

_____

_____

_____

PERSONAL BIRTHDATE NUMBER: _____

HIGHER LAW _____

SPIRITUAL _____ PHYSICAL _____

LOVE _____ EMOTIONAL _____

WISDOM _____ MENTAL _____

COLLECTIVE _____ WILL _____

Like Hitchcock, Spielberg has three twos in his numerology chart. Two is the number of creative drama, conflict and tension. Spielberg's early films, such as *Duel* (1971), *Jaws* (1975) and *Close Encounters of the Third Kind* (1977), were among the most tense and griping cinematic creations of the 1970s. Audiences were compelled to watch Spielberg's extraordinary art of build-up and suspense. Comparison with Hitchcock was inevitable.

Again like Hitchcock, Spielberg has three threes in his numerology chart. Three threes is often a symbol for energy, creativity, enterprise, adventure and wit. Steven Spielberg entertained cinema audiences with a trilogy of exciting, lively and humorous adventures, *Raiders of the Lost Ark* (1981), *Indiana Jones and the Temple of Doom* (1984) and *Indiana Jones and the Last Crusade* (1989).

The numerology charts of Hitchcock and Spielberg bear many striking resemblances. The powerful concentration of the numbers one, two and three in both charts represents a potential of original creativity and inventive impact. Spielberg has only one absent number, the number five. This absence is made up for slightly by the presence of five ones.

Otherwise, his chart is reasonably well balanced, particularly with the appearance of two nines—a symbol for The Watcher and for Higher Self. The spiritual potential of Steven Spielberg's numerology chart is also quite prominent, and may well come into play even more as the years march on.

NAME: _____

_____

_____

_____

_____

PERSONAL NAME NUMBER: _____

DATE OF BIRTH: _____

_____

_____

_____

_____

PERSONAL BIRTHDATE NUMBER: _____

HIGHER LAW _____

SPIRITUAL _____   PHYSICAL _____

LOVE _____   EMOTIONAL _____

WISDOM _____   MENTAL _____

COLLECTIVE _____   WILL _____

A QUICK REFERENCE GUIDE TO THE POTENTIAL OF YOUR NUMBERS

- **One**—A masculine, dynamic, progressive potential. An inventive, creative influence that promotes inspiration, ambition and adventure. Other associations include the physical body, Sun, kundalini, climax, birth, rebirth, life-force, Monad and pioneer.

- **Two**—A feminine, nurturing, unifying potential. Promotes feeling, empathy, intuition and instinct. Romance, soul and healing, creativity, imagination and the unconscious flow freely. Duality of night and day, positive and negative, masculine and feminine is symbolized by this number, which has a potential for both contrasts and union. Two is linked to the emotional body.

- **Three**—A masculine potential that promotes knowledge, reason and intellect. Three activates mind, thought, concepts and ideas. Rational, intellectual, academic, analytical, linguistic left-brain qualities are common. Three can inspire lively, active, progressive, optimistic and outgoing natures. Three is linked to the mental body.

- **Four**—A firm, feminine potential that promotes will, endeavour, commitment and application. Four facilitates practical, up-front, reliable, trustworthy characteristics. Four is a Mother Earth energy, good for building, supporting, and as a foundation. Four inspires the practical romantic. Four is a personal dynamo.

- **Five**—A masculine potential with collective connections—creative, versatile, unconventional and progressive. Five inspires travel, communication, adventure, new horizons. Five feeds the communicator, artist and world citizen. It also fuels talents, charisma and magnetism.

- **Six**—A feminine potential that promotes an appetite for wisdom and for knowing. Six stimulates an interest in beauty, art, composition, geometry and design. Aesthetics, principles, morals and ethics are often evident. Meaning, purpose and direction are vital to life.

- **Seven**—A masculine potential that promotes ambition associated with the thinker, philosopher and mystic. Brotherhood, community, Oneness and Cosmic Consciousness are traditionally linked with seven, which also values and promotes service, teaching, invention and truth. Seven inspires conduct, dignity and knighthood.

- **Eight**—A feminine potential that networks, circuits, connects and organizes. Eight inspires energy, dynamism, endeavour and pursuit. Eight lights up the spiritual, psychic and primordial. The influence of eight supports healers, psychics, mediums, visionaries and spiritual teachers.

- **Nine**—A neutral, balanced potential that feeds universal truth, cosmic law and pure perception. Nine is a symbol for the Higher Self, the Divine Spark, the *I am* and the perfected part of us. Dignity, honour, conduct, service, leadership and the watching mechanism are all inspired by number nine.

CELEBRITY NUMBER PROFILES

Number One People

Mikhail Gorbachev	—	2 March 1931
Martin Luther King	—	15 January 1929
Yoko Ono	—	18 February 1934
Emile Zola	—	2 April 1840
Billy Graham	—	7 November 1918
Emily Brontë	—	30 July 1818
Jimmy Connors	—	2 September 1952
Queen Elizabeth I	—	7 September 1533
Sammy Davis Jr	—	8 December 1925
Mother Teresa	—	27 August 1910
Sean Connery	—	25 August 1930
Prince Andrew	—	19 February 1960
Florence Nightingale	—	12 May 1820
Charles Chaplin	—	16 April 1889

Number Two People

Julie Andrews	—	1 October 1935
Princess Anne	—	15 August 1950
Sir Edmund Hillary	—	20 July 1919
Diana Ross	—	26 March 1893

Ronnie Corbett	—	4 December 1930
Madonna	—	16 August 1958
Paul Getty	—	15 December 1892
Isadora Duncan	—	27 May 1878
Edgar Allan Poe	—	19 January 1809
Shirley Williams	—	27 July 1930
Shirley Bassey	—	8 January 1937
Franco Zefferelli	—	12 February 1923
Ingrid Bergman	—	29 August 1915
Wolfgang Amadeus Mozart	—	27 January 1756
Anne Brontë	—	17 January 1820
Prince Philip	—	10 June 1921
Ronald Reagan	—	6 February 1911

Number Three People

T. E. Lawrence	—	15 August 1888
Amy Johnson	—	1 July 1903
Tommy Steele	—	17 December 1936
Gore Vidal	—	3 October 1925
Sir Alec Guinness	—	2 April 1914
Judy Garland	—	10 June 1922
Charles Dickens	—	7 February 1812
Jane Austen	—	16 December 1775
Mia Farrow	—	9 February 1945
Edward Kennedy	—	22 February 1932
Dionne Warwick	—	12 December 1941
Faye Dunaway	—	14 January 1941
Katharine Hepburn	—	9 November 1909
Audrey Hepburn	—	4 May 1929
David Bowie	—	8 January 1947
Mary Quant	—	11 February 1934
Salvador Dali	—	11 May 1904

Roald Dahl   —   13 September 1916
Indira Gandhi   —   19 November 1917

Number Four People

Woody Allen   —   1 December 1935
Margaret Thatcher   —   13 October 1925
Sir Thomas Beecham   —   29 April 1879
Duchess of York   —   15 October 1959
Paul McCartney   —   18 June 1942
Lady Astor   —   19 May 1879
Martina Navratilova   —   18 October 1956
Anne Bancroft   —   17 September 1931
Sir Harold Wilson   —   11 March 1916
Dorothy L. Sayers   —   13 June 1893
Andre Previn   —   6 April 1929
Queen Elizabeth, the
  Queen Mother   —   4 August 1900
Frank Sinatra   —   12 December 1915
Dolly Parton   —   19 January 1946
Luciano Pavarotti   —   12 October 1935
Barbara Stanwyck   —   16 July 1907
Mark Twain   —   30 November 1835
Douglas Fairbanks Jr   —   9 December 1909

Number Five People

Helen Keller   —   27 June 1880
Earl Mountbatten   —   25 June 1900
Abraham Lincoln   —   12 February 1809
Clare Francis   —   17 April 1946
Victor Borge   —   3 January 1909
Rudolf Nureyev   —   17 March 1938

Henry Winkler   —   30 October 1945
Joan Fontaine   —   22 October 1917
Sir Arthur Conan Doyle—   22 May 1859
Charlotte Brontë   —   21 April 1816
Gustav Holst   —   21 September 1874
Theodore Roosevelt —   27 October 1858

Number Six People

Tony Hancock   —   3 May 1924
Glenda Jackson   —   9 May 1936
Edward Heath   —   9 July 1916
John Lennon   —   9 October 1940
Fred Astaire   —   10 May 1899
Esther Rantzen   —   22 June 1940
Michael Caine   —   14 March 1933
Meryl Streep   —   22 June 1949
Peter Ustinov   —   16 April 1921
Twiggy   —   19 September 1949
Richard Nixon   —   9 January 1913
Harold Pinter   —   10 October 1930
Elizabeth Fry   —   21 May 1780
Roman Polanski   —   18 August 1933
Stevie Wonder   —   13 May 1950
Susan Hampshire   —   12 May 1942

Number Seven People

Queen Elizabeth II —   21 April 1926
George Bush   —   12 June 1924
Princess of Wales   —   1 July 1961
Bob Dylan   —   24 May 1941
Marilyn Monroe   —   1 June 1926

Alfred Adler	—	7 February 1870
Dame Margot Fonteyn	—	18 May 1919
Rudolph Valentino	—	6 May 1895
George Eliot (Mary Ann Evans)	—	22 November 1819
Peter Sellers	—	8 September 1925
Franz Liszt	—	22 October 1811
Emmeline Pankhurst	—	14 July 1858
Leonard Nimoy	—	26 March 1931
Sir Winston Churchill	—	30 November 1874

Number Eight People

Jane Fonda	—	21 December 1937
Gerald Ford	—	14 July 1913
Nancy Reagan	—	6 July 1921
Oscar Wilde	—	16 October 1854
Aretha Franklin	—	25 March 1942
Sir Laurence Olivier	—	22 May 1907
Elizabeth Taylor	—	27 February 1932
George Orwell	—	25 June 1903
Dame Anna Neagle	—	20 October 1904
Pablo Picasso	—	25 October 1881
Barbra Streisand	—	24 April 1942
Alexander Graham Bell	—	3 March 1847
Mary Baker Eddy	—	16 July 1821
Neil Armstrong	—	5 August 1930
Daphne du Maurier	—	13 May 1907

Number Nine People

Dustin Hoffman	—	8 August 1937
Shirley MacLaine	—	24 April 1934
Lord Baden-Powell	—	22 February 1857
Joan Baez	—	9 January 1941
Francis Bacon	—	22 January 1561
H. W. Longfellow	—	27 February 1807
Gracie Fields	—	9 January 1898
Mahatma Gandhi	—	2 October 1869
Virginia Woolf	—	25 January 1882
Sir Robert Walpole	—	26 August 1676
Neville Chamberlain	—	18 March 1869
Kiri Te Kanawa	—	6 March 1944
General Franco	—	4 December 1892
Orson Welles	—	6 May 1915

NAME: _____

_____

_____

_____

_____

PERSONAL NAME NUMBER: _____

DATE OF BIRTH: _____

_____

_____

_____

_____

PERSONAL BIRTHDATE NUMBER: _____

HIGHER LAW _____

SPIRITUAL _____ PHYSICAL _____

LOVE _____ EMOTIONAL _____

WISDOM _____ MENTAL _____

COLLECTIVE _____ WILL _____

NAME: _____

_____

_____

_____

_____

PERSONAL NAME NUMBER: _____

DATE OF BIRTH: _____

_____

_____

_____

_____

PERSONAL BIRTHDATE NUMBER: _____

HIGHER LAW _____

SPIRITUAL _____   PHYSICAL _____

LOVE _____   EMOTIONAL _____

WISDOM _____   MENTAL _____

COLLECTIVE _____   WILL _____

NAME: _____

_____

_____

_____

_____

PERSONAL NAME NUMBER: _____

DATE OF BIRTH: _____

_____

_____

_____

_____

PERSONAL BIRTHDATE NUMBER: _____

HIGHER LAW _____

SPIRITUAL _____   PHYSICAL _____

LOVE _____   EMOTIONAL _____

WISDOM _____   MENTAL _____

COLLECTIVE _____   WILL _____